WITHDRAWN

English Courts
of Law

H.G.Hanbury
D.C.M.Yardley

English Courts
of Law

Fifth edition
prepared by D.C.M.Yardley

Oxford New York Toronto Melbourne
OXFORD UNIVERSITY PRESS
1979

Oxford University Press, Walton Street, Oxford OX2 6DP

OXFORD LONDON GLASGOW
NEW YORK TORONTO MELBOURNE WELLINGTON
KUALA LUMPUR SINGAPORE JAKARTA HONG KONG TOKYO
DELHI BOMBAY CALCUTTA MADRAS KARACHI
NAIROBI DAR ES SALAAM CAPE TOWN

First edition in the Home University Library *1944*
Second edition 1953
Third edition 1960
Fourth edition by D. C. M. Yardley in
Oxford Paperbacks University Series *1967*
Fifth edition 1979

British Library Cataloguing in Publication Data

Hanbury, Harold Greville
    English courts of law. – 5th ed.
    1. Courts – England – History
    I. Title   II. Yardley, David Charles Miller
    347'.42'0109   KD6850   79–40231

ISBN 0–19–219139–X
ISBN 0–19–289126–X Pbk

*Typeset by Filmtype Services Ltd, Scarborough and
printed in Great Britain by Cox & Wyman Ltd,
Reading*

Contents

Preface to the fifth edition

This little book first appeared in 1944, and it provided a stimulating and colourful account of the courts, the judges, and the legal profession in the twentieth century, all set in their historical context. Indeed, well over half the book was concerned with the history of the English legal system, and Professor Hanbury made bold to include many examples taken from old substantive law to illustrate his comments upon the functions of the courts. This was no dull, prosaic description of our modern courts, and the exact details of precise jurisdiction were never allowed to obtrude unduly. For such technical details supplementary reading is needed, and the book has always contained a selection of further reading to be consulted by the reader. The great value of the work, however, has been in its broad sweep of the whole field occupied by the judicial system, assisting the reader to master the reason and meaning of its development, and often driving home the points made with striking metaphors. The volume has been a work of literature as well as of law, and many students have welcomed the aid towards understanding which has been provided for them in so small a compass and in such a pleasurable way.

Professor Hanbury revised the book for two further editions. But a dozen years ago, when a fourth edition was required, he felt that the difficulties of keeping up with rapid modern developments were too great for one no longer regularly engaged in law teaching. Accordingly he did me the honour to ask me to prepare the new edition. I approached the task with trepidation, but was much assisted by the generosity of Professor Hanbury in handing over to me the notes he had made since he produced the third edition in 1960, and by his constant encouragement. As the time for a fifth edition has drawn near, and as the alterations required for the book have become more substantial, Professor Hanbury has suggested that this new edition should appear under our joint names as authors. My appreciation of this gesture is only equalled by my wish to acknowledge here the many ideas he has put forward for possible incorporation in this latest version of the book.

The past twelve years have been marked by a veritable avalanche of new statute law, part of it occasioned by the substantial efforts of the English Law Commission (which had started work only shortly before the publication of the fourth edition of this book), but much of it being the vehicle for major reforms of the English legal system recommended by diverse bodies, and notably by the Report in 1969 of the Royal Commission on Assizes and Quarter Sessions, chaired by Lord Beeching. The Acts of Parliament relevant to the subject of this book are too numerous to list here, but there have been no fewer than four Administration of Justice Acts and two Criminal Justice Acts since the last edition appeared, as well as three Local Government Acts, a Juries Act, a Tribunals and Inquiries Act, a Justices of the Peace Act, a Solicitors Act, a European Communities Act, and a whole crop of other statutes which *inter alia* affect the functions of the courts in a variety of ways. But overshadowing all these measures has been the Courts Act 1971, which alone has effected a major restructuring of both criminal and civil courts. At the time of preparing the fourth edition of this book the 1870s stood out as the most important era of reform of the English court system since the reign of Henry II, and the Judicature Act 1873, which was concerned almost entirely with civil courts, was the culmination of a steady acceleration of reforming measures during the reign of Queen Victoria. It is now plain that the reforms of the 1970s are as significant as those of a century earlier, and perhaps more wideranging in that they cover the whole spectrum of courts, civil and criminal.

It was thus abundantly clear that a new edition of this book was needed. Most of the historical material in the fourth edition has remained as valid as ever, though I have attempted to amend a few passages in the light of suggestions made to me and of some recent research. I have also taken account of what is now the more generally recognized vindication of Richard III. But equally most of the account of the modern system was badly out of date. As well as dealing with modern statutes, I have tried to refer to the progress of juristic and political opinions on sovereignty. I have also taken account of the many recent cases in which the courts have asserted their powers of judicial control over executive action, of improved remedies for achieving judicial review, and of the increase in extra-judicial remedies, especially by resort to 'ombudsmen'. Among the many other modern developments referred to are the modernization of the jury system; the new arrangements for training and examination of intending solicitors and barristers; the effects of the United Kingdom's membership of the European Economic Community, and of possible devolution of some power to Scotland and Wales; and the celebrated case in 1972 by which we were all reminded of the powers of the Official Solicitor. In the last edition, for reasons of consistency, I deliberately retained references to the Court of King's Bench and the King's Bench Division throughout the book. But now that we have celebrated the Silver Jubilee of Queen Elizabeth II it has seemed to me to be unrealistic not to refer to the Queen's Bench Division as it exists today. Accordingly I have adopted the expedient of using the older names in the earlier chapters, and then moving on to refer to the Queen's Bench Division, and indeed to the Queen rather than King, in those parts of the book which expressly relate to the present day. In the result a good proportion of the book has had to be rewritten, though many of the historical passages remain substantially as they left the pen of the original author, and I have tried to ensure that the whole book retains its characteristic flavour. I hope that the finished work will not disgrace the high standard set by Professor Hanbury thirty-five years ago.

D.C.M.Y.
Oxford, 23 March 1979

1 The content of the law

On the whole the judicial office in England stands in high popular regard. Were a critic of our institutions to hint that the fountain of justice is impure, that an English judge is capable of accepting a bribe, or being turned aside from pursuing his rightful path by executive pressure or favour, it is unlikely that he would be believed. Through centuries of service, our judges have come to be associated with all that is finest in our national life. But veneration is a sentiment which may injure its object, unless canalized by discrimination. So high is the standard of judicial probity and morality that there is a danger that the nature of the judicial function may in some respects be misunderstood. By a paraphrase of Falstaff, judges are moral, but they are not the reason why morals exist in other men. In a word, their function is the enunciation and enforcement of law, not of morality.

A demarcation of the frontiers of these two realms would appear desirable. But this is impracticable, for much territory is common to both. Though law and morals do not coincide, there are many points of intersection. Respect for human life, for human reputation, for the sanctity of contract, are enjoined by both. But there are wide tracts of morality into which law cannot prudently intrude. For morality prescribes a course of conduct both positive and negative; it bids men not merely to eschew evil, but actively to do good. But the precepts of law are mainly, though by no means entirely, negative. 'Thou shalt not kill, but need'st not strive officiously to keep alive.' A man who stands idly by, and watches a baby drown in two feet of water, when he could save it with no further inconvenience to himself than of wetting his hands, gravely offends the code of morals, but not that of law. Law does not aspire to call forth the ideal qualities of human nature.

Again, much even of the negative field of morality is avoided by law, for much of sin dwells in the realms of thought, and as the

Mohammedan saying has it, 'None but God and I know what is in my heart.' Thus the Seven Deadly Sins are not necessarily deadly crimes as well. The law will not take cognizance of them unless they manifest themselves in certain forms of practical action. It will not punish gluttony, unless it render a man drunk and disorderly, or unfit to drive a motor vehicle; or wrath, unless it take effect in the infliction of death or wounds; or sloth, unless it lead to the evasion of the payment of taxes. A comparative study of legal systems in different countries and at different periods will of course reveal striking differences of viewpoint as to the extent to which the field of law should endeavour to invade the field of morals. Thus adultery is not in England a crime; it is not even a civil wrong, though it is true that the common law action for enticement was open to a wife or husband, the affections of whose spouse had been alienated by a rival, until this cause of action was abolished by Parliament in 1970. But some legal systems have made it criminal, and visited it with the severest penalities. Thus in the grim times of Cromwell it was capital; and readers of Hawthorne's *The Scarlet Letter* will recollect that the early laws of Massachusetts condemned a convicted adulteress to stand some hours on a platform, the cynosure of the censorious public gaze, and thereafter for ever. to wear the letter A worked in scarlet on her breast.

Some legal systems have gone yet further, in using the criminal law to prohibit acts of which the immorality is debatable. Such experiments have generally proved useless. As an eminent American judge once put it, it must always be a mistake to harness the criminal law to the object of discouraging acts which their perpetrators do not think morally wrong. The habitual disregard shown in England for the Sunday Observance Act of Charles II, which was not repealed until 1969, by the Statute Law (Repeals) Act, and in some of the States of America for the laws prohibiting the sale of alcoholic liquors, provide obvious illustrations of the truth of his estimate. But the experiments have been in many cases even worse than useless, for contempt for one law passed at the instance of a vocal and fanatical minority, who have an erroneous view of the real content of morality, cannot but inculcate contempt for law in general.

But there is another side to the picture. Law must take cognizance of many things with which morality has nothing to do. For the masons of law employ cement of a type which the merchants of morality view with indifference. No modern criminal code could afford to omit a law of treason, and of other political offences. In fact, the great historian of criminal law, Stephen, recommended that political offences should meet with severer punishment, on the ground that the cohesion of society must at all costs be safeguarded; and it is noteworthy that the Murder (Abolition of Death Penalty) Act 1965, which abolishes capital punishment for the crime of murder, leaves it as the penalty for treason. He who rises against the government in power is legally a traitor, and yet among those who have done this very thing are some of the heroes of history. For morality prescribes obedience, but not blind obedience, to lawful human authority. There comes a point, when a government declares right to be wrong, and wrong right, at which obedience ceases to be a virtue, and resistance becomes a moral duty.

Laws establishing political offences are postulated by social security, but other offences are continually added by social complexity. We shall see that there is a sharp line of cleavage between indictable and non-indictable crimes, and that many of the latter carry with them no moral stigma whatsoever. The driving force that erects such acts into crimes is the need for a certain amount of uniformity in human relationships. The great case of *Institute of Patent Agents* v. *Lockwood* in 1894, whose ramifications involved the consideration by the House of Lords of the most vital problems in constitutional law, arose out of the fulfilment by Parliament of just this need. For it was realized that it was in the interests of society that the number of patent agents should be restricted, and so by a regulation made by the President of the Board of Trade, under the Patents and Designs Act 1888, it was laid down that a man intending to practise as a patent agent must go through certain formalities, including registration with the Board of Trade. But it would be idle to prescribe this course of conduct without also providing machinery for its enforcement. The regulation left it uncertain whether it intended the method of coercion of a recalcitrant patent agent to be a criminal prosecution or a civil action for an interdict.[1] The House of Lords decided that the former type of

[1] This is the Scottish counterpart of injunction, as to which see p. 103.

proceeding was proper; Lockwood had, by practising without registration, committed what was technically a crime, punishable by a small fine.

In many civil matters, also, such as the conditions for the validity of a will, though the voice of morality is silent, yet a ruling by the law is indispensable.

The proper function, then, of judges, is the enunciation and enforcement of law, and not of morals. Law cannot be more accurately defined than as the sum of rules of human conduct which the Courts will enforce. Most cases coming before judges for decision partake of the nature of disputes. The basic division of the whole province of law is into public and private law. Cases falling within the former are those in which one of the disputants is the Crown, in its character of chief executive and chief guardian of public order. Foremost in the field of public law is criminal law. In every criminal prosecution, the party in whose name the law must necessarily be set in motion is the Crown, for we shall see that one of the great principles established by Henry II was that a crime is to be looked upon as an offence, not against an individual—to be bought off, as in primitive law, with a money payment—but against the King's Peace, and the whole community who live under its sure shield. But though in every criminal case the Crown must be a party, the converse is not true. For there are many civil cases wherein the Crown is concerned, whether as defendant or, more rarely, as plaintiff. Proceedings by a subject against the Crown are regulated by the Crown Proceedings Act 1947, which, subject to certain exceptions, places Government Departments on the same footing, for purposes of litigation, as private individuals. In most cases of tort committed against a subject by a servant of the Crown, and in cases of contract, other than those relating to service under the Crown, and those in which the Crown purports to fetter its own future executive action, which it has been judicially declared incompetent to do, the subject can bring an ordinary action against the appropriate Government Department. The legislation of the 1914–18 war which gave to the Crown its requisitioning powers was prolific of litigation, and the 1939–45 war also produced its crop, in spite of the greater comprehensiveness and precision of the legislation concerned. An instance of a case in which the Crown may appear in the role of plaintiff is that in which it sues to recover damages against a trespasser on the foreshore, which is by law Crown property.

These cases belong not to criminal law, but to the other great branch of public law known as constitutional law, in which is bound up administrative law. Some cases in constitutional law are of great complexity, for with the growth of Parliament's practice of delegating to the executive the power of making regulations within the scope of statutes laying down the general principles of matters of high policy, the Courts are endowed with the function of determining whether this or that regulation is really within or outside the scope of the statutory provision under which it was made. This function, which is of an ever-increasing importance, involves consideration of the famous *ultra vires* doctrine, discussion of which will be postponed until we come to the theory of the Separation of Powers.

In cases falling within the sphere of private law, both disputants are private individuals. The most important are those arising out of breaches of contract and of tort. Contracts are agreements between two parties, to which those parties must be taken to have intended that the binding force of law should attach. Without a law of contract the easy flow of commercial enterprise would be impossible. This is no reproach to the commercial morality of the age, for though two parties to an agreement may nourish in their hearts a deeply implanted sense of honour, yet they cannot have the prophetic power to visualize all future eventualities which may upset their calculations, and only a trained commercial judge can be expected to decide what the position of agreement may be, in the light of changed circumstances. The field of tort overlaps that of crime; thus assault, libel, conspiracy are both crimes and torts. But many torts fall right outside the field of crime. Thus if a man, however innocently, exercises over another man's property powers consistent only with the legal right to its possession, he has committed a tort of wrongful interference, and may find himself, though of course guilty of no crime, liable to reimburse the owner to the extent of the full value of the property.

The vital difference between criminal and civil liability lies in the nature of the sanction, the understanding of which is as important to the student of law as is that of an axiom to a student of geometry. A legal sanction is a result which will follow, with such a degree of certainty as is consistent with human fallibility, non-compliance with a rule of law. The sanction of criminal law is punitive; the object of a criminal prosecution is the punishment of the accused. But that of civil law is compensation for the injured party. If a man brings an action for breach of contract, he is asking the judge to order the other party, in certain cases, to carry it out according to its terms, and in most cases to pay damages. Likewise the object of an action for tort is either the recovery of damages, or an order of the Court, known as an injunction, forbidding the defendant to begin or continue the injury. A second difference lies in the inherence of the power to waive the sanction. As crime is a wrong against the Crown, and a prosecution must be in the name of the Crown, it follows that the Crown can refuse to pursue the matter. If a thief picks my pocket and I report the matter to the police, and the thief is arrested and put on trial, the Crown may suddenly, without any explanation to me, stop the trial, or may, after his conviction and sentence, award him a free pardon. But the Crown is not concerned with a tort or breach of contract, unless actually suing or being sued as a real party. Nothing can save a defendant against whom a judgement has been recorded from the obligation to pay damages unless the plaintiff magnanimously forgoes his rights.

It is true of most cases that come before judges, that they are disputes, but it is not true of all. Judges are sometimes called upon to act as administrators rather than as referees, for an executor will often come to the Court simply to ask for directions as to the distribution of an estate under an obscure will. Every will must, as a matter of course, first undergo the process known as probate, and matters concerning its validity may fall to be determined by a judge of the High Court (Family Division if the matter is non-contentious, or Chancery Division if it is contentious). The sanction which enforces the statutory rule that a will must be attested by two witnesses is the sanction of nullity; that is to say, without due attestation the will is null and void.

Having passed in review the material on which the Courts work, we must now inquire how that material has been collected. We are face to face with the important problem of the sources of the law. This subject has given rise to more intricate and protracted controversy than any other subject in jurisprudence. The great German jurist Savigny described law as the product of the common consciousness of the people. On the other hand Austin, the father of English analytical jurisprudence, viewed all law as essentially a command of the sovereign power. Modern writers, in treating these two standpoints as irreconcilable with one another, have created a difficulty where none exists. Each is correct within its own sphere. Savigny was approaching the matter historically, in an endeavour to excavate the early German tribal rules and customs from under the superstructure of Roman Law, which had been received into medieval Germany. But Austin was not primarily interested in history; though intensely learned in it, and keenly appreciative of all its lessons, he regarded it, from the point of view of jurisprudence, chiefly as a storehouse of illustration. He was concerned with the phenomena of contemporary government. In his eyes, the appropriate subject-matter of jurisprudence consists of positive laws, that is to say, rules set by men, as political superiors, to other men. This definition postulated that his account of law should be prefaced by the determination of the nature of sovereignty, for all law must flow from the sovereign power. His famous theory of sovereignty is expressed in the following words: 'If a determinate human superior, not in a habit of obedience to a like superior, receive habitual obedience from the bulk of a given society, that determinate superior is sovereign in that society, and the society (including the superior) is a society political and independent.' He emphasizes that no man, or body of men, can be truly sovereign unless fulfilling both the positive and the negative requirements; that they receive habitual obedience from the bulk of the society is no whit more important than that there exist no other superior to whom they themselves yield obedience. Governments are classified according to the composition of the sovereign power. They fall into two categories, and two only, monarchy and aristocracy. In the case of the former, the sovereign power resides in one man; in the case of the latter, it resides in several. While monarchies are uniform, aristocracies fall into two subdivisions according to the numbers of those making up the sovereign. Where the numbers are few, the government is an oligarchy; where they are many, it is a democracy. The term 'limited monarchy' is meaningless, for on the scope of the sovereign power there can be no legal, though there may be many moral and practical, limitations. A limited monarchy is, from the legal point of view, not a monarchy at all, but an aristocracy. He correctly classified the constitution of Great Britain as that of a democracy, though he erred as to his location of the sovereign power. For he attributed it to the threefold authority of King, House of Lords, and Electorate. Dickens, in his picture of the reception given by Mr. Gregsbury, M.P., to the deputation headed by his old friend, Mr. Pugstyles, has brought home to us, with all the force of his inimitable satire, that the conduct of an elected member of the House of Commons cannot in any way be controlled by his constituents, except only through the fear that they will withhold their votes from him at the next election. This fear, to the aspirant to a permanent Parliamentary career, is a very real one, and Dicey struck the right balance when he placed the legal sovereignty in King, Lords, and Commons, and the political sovereignty in the Electorate. That is to say, though the legal power of Parliament is unlimited, the Electorate are sure to have, in fact, the final word, for a government which persuades Parliament to pass unpopular legislation will find itself at last rejected by the popular vote.

Austin's thesis is one long assertion of the legal omnipotence of the sovereign power. No law laid down by the sovereign can be legally unjust; courts of law are bound simply to apply it, irrespective of its goodness or its badness. Until the modern shift of juristic opinion in England towards the views of Kelsen and Professor Hart[2], who may be described as in essence Neo-Austinians, much criticism of Austin, or rather of theories wrongly attributed to him, had been made on the ground that he insists on force. Hart stresses that much law is obeyed simply out of habit, and anyway, as Markby[3] so sensibly pointed out nearly a century ago, Austin's views provide no suitable theme for political polemics. His aim was simply to show us the structure of government as it actually exists, and those who ransack his pages for any hidden social philosophy will have a barren search. Of course it is clear that in fact a sovereign who resorts to tyranny will ultimately cease to receive the habitual obedience of the bulk of the community, and so will yield his place to another man, or body of men, who can in fact

---

[2] See especially H. L. A. Hart, *The Concept of Law* (Clarendon Law Series).
[3] Author of *Elements of Law* (sixth ed., Oxford, 1905).

command it, and from the moment at which they begin to command it.

Without a thorough grounding in Austinian principles, no student can hope to understand the British Constitution, for its very foundation is the omnipotence, or, to employ a word preferred by several historians, omnicompetence, of the sovereign. Of the system of government in his own country, Austin gave us a completely faithful portrait. He was far less happy in his attempts to fit his theory of sovereignty into forms of federal government. Now a federal system postulates a nice division of powers between the central and local spheres of authority, by a fundamental law. In such a constitution, the existence of a sovereign in the Austinian sense is impossible. For if any body within the State is endowed with the power to change the fundamental law, the federal balance at once becomes more than precarious, for it is subject to alteration, or extinction, at the whim of the sovereign legislature. If the federal balance is to be safeguarded, it is essential that amendments to the fundamental law should be effected only in one of two ways: (a) by some *body outside the State*, or (b) by some *extraordinary force, or conjunction of forces, within the State*. Method (a) is adopted in Canada, for though by the British North America (No. 2) Act 1949, the Canadian Parliament is given a power of amending the constitution, it does not yet extend to some of the most important matters: (i) those assigned exclusively to the legislatures of the Provinces; (ii) privileges as regards education and language, (iii) annual sessions, and, in normal circumstances, quinquennial duration of Parliament; changes in these three can still, under the Statute of Westminster 1931, be effected only by the Westminster Parliament, though efforts are currently being made in Canada to find an acceptable internal substitute for this external method of constitutional amendment. Method (b) is adopted in the United States, for under the Constitution of 1787, amendments to that consitution can be passed only through a two-thirds majority in both Houses of Congress, ratified by three-quarters of the States. The Parliament at Ottawa and the Congress at Washington are, to use Dicey's phrase, non-sovereign legislative bodies. It follows that if a man is prosecuted for disobeying one of their enactments he can plead that it was unconstitutional, that is to say, contrary to one of the provisions of the fundamental law, and if the court endorses his view he will be acquitted, and the enactment will, in effect, lose its validity. But the British Parliament is completely sovereign, and there is no such thing as an unconstitutional Act of Parliament, because we have no touchstone of constitutionality. We have no such thing as fundamental laws; Magna Carta or the Bill of Rights could be repealed by Parliament as easily as can an enactment on the most trivial of matters.

Those who have argued that the United Kingdom's accession to the European Community, which was given effect in law by the European Communities Act 1972, has resulted in some loss of our Parliamentary sovereignty have been in error. Although the Community institutions are thereby empowered to make regulations on various matters which are automatically binding in the United Kingdom, nothing has infringed the right of Parliament to repeal the 1972 Act (as indeed might have happened if the majority vote in the referendum held on this issue in June 1975 had been in favour of such a change). The case of *Chester* v. *Bateson* in 1920 provides an apt illustration both of the omnipotence of Parliament and of the absence of fundamental laws, and at the same time lifts the curtain a little on the doctrine of *ultra vires*, of whose existence a hint has already been given, and which must later be more fully revealed. The Defence of the Realm Act 1914, the counterpart of the Emergency Powers Act 1939, gave to Ministers a latitude in making regulations which was indispensable for the successful prosecution of the war. The Minister of Munitions, in order to secure the proximity of workers to their work, issued a regulation that no landlord should take proceedings for ejecting a munition worker from any dwelling in the vicinity of that work, and prescribing penal sanctions for non-compliance. It was argued that the regulation could not stand, in that it was contrary to the provision of Magna Carta, 'to none will we deny justice'. Lord Darling disposed of this contention on the vital ground that there is nothing sacrosanct about Magna Carta; provided only that the regulation was consistent with the powers of legislation delegated by Parliament to the Minister, its validity was equal with that of Parliament itself. But he ruled that the Minister had in fact been over-optimistic in his interpretation of the Act in question; nothing in it confided to him so drastic a power as that of depriving the King's subjects of their elementary right of access to the courts, and the regulation was, therefore, of no effect.

Non-lawyers are sometimes shocked to learn that in England, the home of freedom, we live, in law, under a despotism. But paradoxically, the completeness of that despotism is in fact the very coping-stone of our democracy. For the most potent of the three component parts of the sovereign power consists of the elected representatives of the people. They represent every shade of opinion. The result is that if a measure is at all controversial it is sure of protracted debate in the House of Commons, wherein it is thoroughly discussed from every angle. And even when the measure has withstood this ordeal, it has, unless it is certified by the Speaker as a Money Bill, still to undergo the scrutiny of the House of Lords, which can, under the Parliament Act 1949, suspend it for a period of one year. By another paradox, while the representative character of the Commons forms one half of the safeguard against precipitate or tyrannous legislation, it is precisely the non-representative character of the Lords that provides the other half, in that it enables them to take a dispassionate view. Some measures, however, are not controversial at all, but are in the nature of desperate remedies for admitted evils. It is here that the advantage of an absolute sovereign is most apparent, for it makes it possible for immediate effect to be given to the will of the people. In 1936 the Abdication Act was passed through all its stages within twenty-four hours. If a constitutional change in the United States is desired by every interest in the nation, by Congress, and by the President, it can be brought about only by an Amendment to the Constitution, which must inevitably take some time, as was demonstrated by the period that elapsed between the first move to repeal the Eighteenth (Prohibition) Amendment and its ultimate and unlamented demise.

We may lament that Austin took so restricted a view of the province of the science of jurisprudence, and did not follow up his picture of the legal sovereignty of Parliament with some account of the way in which the constitution functions in practice; that he did not, like his far more famous contemporary and fellow-utilitarian, Bentham, go on to deal with the philosophy of legislation. But we must remember two things. Firstly, to each his trade; Austin was essentially an academic exponent, Bentham a practical reformer. Secondly, when Austin wrote, much that is to us obvious was still obscure. He wrote in the first half of the nineteenth century; in the latter part of the eighteenth, Blackstone, the great commentator, who rivalled the achievement of Bracton, five hundred years earlier, of writing a comprehensive account of the laws of England, and who won everlasting and deserved renown by reason alike of the profundity of his learning and the elegance and dignity of his style, was enunciating to his classes at Oxford the tenet that then had a firm hold on juristic opinion, that a statute contravening the moral law was null and void. Small wonder that the accurate mind of Austin should be preoccupied with the dire necessity for dispelling the mists of ethical suasion with the salubrious wind of legal realism.

But Austin's framework is of amply sufficient capacity to enable us to form an accurate view of the sources of English law. It is commonly said that these are three—statute law, common law, and equity. The distinction between the two last-named may be postponed until a later stage; both grew through the same agency, judicial precedent, while statute law is the creature of Parliament. But Austin quite correctly insists that for all law there is but one original source, for all law flows from the command of the sovereign power. The sovereign may make laws directly, through an Act of Parliament, or indirectly, through regulations made by a subordinate authority to whom he has delegated legislative power, or through the decisions of judges, which he permits them to render, and which he will himself enforce.

Judical precedent plays a very large part in the growth of English law. Though the volume of legislation continually increases, there are still large tracts which no statute has traversed. That 'malice aforethought' is necessary to constitute the crime of murder, that contracts must be performed or damages paid in default, that a man must not write of his neighbour words which tend to lower his reputation in the eyes of right-thinking persons: these fundamental rules of law are laid down by no statute, but are the creatures of judicial decision. Our very constitution, as Dicey reminds us, is a 'judge-made constitution'; it does not create the rights of the subject to freedom of the person, of expression, of assembly, but is itself the outcome of those rights, affirmed from the earliest times by courts of justice. The great writ of Habeas Corpus had been in common operation for some centuries before

Parliament thought it necessary to polish and sharpen its machinery by the Habeas Corpus Act of 1679.

It was at one time a matter of controversy whether judges can truly be said to make the law, or whether their function is declaratory. Geldart, in his *Elements of English Law*, has given us an account of the conflicting arguments to which nothing can now be added. But it is doubtful whether judges who disclaimed the function of law-makers were wholly serious in taking so modest a view of their mission, or conscious of the full implications of their repudiation. Invocations, to which certain nineteenth-century judges were addicted, of a recondite body of law reposing 'in the breasts of the judges', a holy mystery hidden from the profane eyes of the barrister, revealed to him only at the moment when his shoulders first felt the impress of the judicial ermine, are explicable only on the hypothesis that devotion of the lips to traditional jargon, long after it has ceased to deceive the heart, dies hard in all professions. Nobody now would seriously deny that the judges do make law. There are many well-established rules of law and equity whose origin we can trace to one particular decision of a court. The doctrine that a purchaser of land with notice of a covenant, restrictive of the use of the land, entered into by his vendor with an adjoining land-owner, is bound by that covenant, was started on its course by *Holmes* v. *Buckley* in 1691. The general proposition that if A has a contract with B, and C, knowing of its existence, persuades B to break it, C is liable in damages for tort to A, was established by *Lumley* v. *Gye* in 1853. In this, as in other fields of thought, we are returning to the relentless logic of Austin. Neither he nor Bentham had any doubt that judges make the law. But they differed widely in their views of the desirability of their doing so. Austin, being interested only in describing what is, and not at all in speculations on what should be, was content with demonstrating the system, but Bentham roundly condemned it. He, the ardent law reformer, would have had all law made by Parliament. But he at once overrated the omniscience of Parliament, and underrated the English dislike of writing down more than the occasion demands. The English habit of mind prefers the fortuitous to the systematic; it prefers to leave problems to be dealt with as they arise; in a word, it prefers judicial precedent to codification, which has seemed indispensable to framers of the legal schemes of most European countries. In certain fields of criminal and commercial law, it is true, experience has pointed the way to a codifying Act, but the Act which can cover all the manifold cases which may arise has yet to be devised.

Expressed in its simplest terms, the theory of judicial precedent is that a decision of a judge, once given, on a question of law, binds subsequent judges in a court of lower rank to decide the same question in the same way. It also normally binds subsequent judges in courts of equal rank, though the ultimate court of appeal, the House of Lords, declared in 1966 that it would in future be prepared to depart from a previous decision where it appears just to do so. Naturally, it is rare to find two cases with exactly the same facts, and it will often be the duty of a judge to decide whether the facts of the case before him are really covered by a previous decision which has been cited to him. He will, in fact, apply to the older case either a widening or a narrowing interpretation.

We shall see that the stream of judicial precedent, like Matthew Arnold's Oxus, was for long 'shorn and parcelled' by the sands of procedural inhibition and rivalry between courts; only within living memory has it burst the bonds of antique forms and become free, through channels cut by skilled judicial engineers, to irrigate the whole territory of human society.

2 The work of Henry II

Three powers of government are necessary to the progress of a State, the legislature, which makes the laws, the executive, which carries out the laws, and performs the work of administration, and the judiciary, which interprets the laws, and decides disputes between the State and its subjects, and between two subjects. The great French jurist Montesquieu, in his immortal *Esprit des Lois*, insisted that these three must be kept separate from one another, for a union of any two of them in the same hands leads inevitably to tyranny. Alexander Hamilton devoured with avidity every page of this great work, and to this appetite is attributable the fact that the doctrine of the separation of powers, though nowhere expressly mentioned in the letter of the American Constitution, permeates its spirit in every line. The functions and powers of Congress are enumerated in the first Article, those of the President in the second, those of the Supreme Court in the third. No one occupying a place of profit under the United States can be a member of either House of Congress; this provision excludes not only the members of the federal judiciary, but also the President and every member of his Cabinet, except the Vice-President, as well as a whole host of minor officials. The legislative powers of Congress are not, as those of the British Parliament, unlimited, but defined by the Constitution, and it often becomes the duty of the Supreme Court to decide whether a piece of legislation is in harmony with that definition. Each of the three great organs has its own sphere; the executive and judiciary are never in any sense at the mercy of the legislature.

But in Great Britain the legislature is legally omnipotent. It could with equal facility resign all its own powers to the executive or abolish the judiciary. By a curious irony, Montesquieu, searching like the children in Maeterlinck's play, for the Blue Bird of Happiness, imagined that it had already taken tangible form in the neighbouring wood, whereas his thought had really called it into being in the Country of the Future. That is to say, abandoning the language of metaphor, the system, whose existence he wrongly ascribed to contemporary England, was destined to see the light for the first time in the United States of America. The framers of the union of the seceded colonies were determined that it should retain the good parts of the British Constitution, and reject the bad. The mother's house was the work of many hands, portions having been built on to it without any unified plan as the need arose; but for the daughter a new house, all of one period, was to be built, after the master-design of Montesquieu.

We are here concerned to describe the house of the mother, and the vicissitudes of its construction. The doctrine of the separation of powers has played no conscious part in the growth of the British Constitution. At times we have been impelled forward by its current, only to be borne back again into our own familiar coves. The following reflections will serve to demonstrate that the three organs are closely interlocked:

(*a*) So far from being spearated from the legislature, the members of the executive form in it a predominant, and at times almost dictatorial, block. It is in practice impossible for any member of the Cabinet to retain office unless he be a member of one or other House of Parliament.

(*b*) The House of Lords is at the same time the highest court of law and the Upper House of the Legislature.

(*c*) The Judicial Committee of the Privy Council, in hearing appeals from those other parts of the Commonwealth from which appeals may still be brought, is acting partly in an executive and partly in a judicial capacity.

In order to explain these and many other prominent features of the English system, it is necessary to turn back the pages of history and examine the medieval Curia Regis. In approaching this study we must remember two things: firstly, the enormous significance of the Norman Conquest; and secondly, which is a corollary of it, the importance of the land law.

'When our gallant Norman foes made this merry land their own, and the Saxons from the Conqueror were flying,' the Conqueror did more than build the Tower of London. It is a matter of vital necessity to assess exactly what he did do, and this cannot be done without forming a mental picture of contemporary events.

Macaulay would have us regard England at the end of 1066 as placed suddenly under the domination of a victorious foreign invader, who seized all her land, which he parcelled out among his Norman followers, and was interested in her only as a larder and storehouse. The interests of England and those of her kings were as the poles apart until the accident of a bad king, who reigned from 1199 to 1216, for the first time drove the Norman barons to make common cause with the English people and made England a nation. On the other hand, Tennyson pictures William as standing on the field of battle at Senlac and uttering his prayer:

> Of one self-stock at first
> Make them again one people—Norman, English
> And English, Norman; we should have a hand
> To grasp the world with, and a foot to stamp it
> Flat.

Which of these estimates contains the truth? The Conqueror did indeed take into his hands all the English land, and divide it among his Barons; his hand was indeed heavy on the English, and Hereward the Wake and his followers have won the aureole of worship which is ever the guerdon of those patriots whose resistance to the oppressor knows no end but death. It is also true that he and the six succeeding kings remained Dukes of Normandy, and probably tended to regard England as an appendage of their Norman Duchy, a feeling which finds an echo in the quite justifiable claim of the Channel Islanders that England belongs to them, rather than they to her. Further, a mark of his insistence on the superiority of Normans over English is to be found in his institution of the murder-fine, whereby collective responsibility for the death of a Norman was placed on the hundred, the small unit of local government within the county. If a person were found dead, and there were no 'presentment of Englishry', that is to say, if the body could not be proved to be that of an Englishman, it was presumed to be that of a Norman, and the hundred was rendered liable to pay a murder-fine.

But there are many pointers in the opposite direction. There is little evidence that the murder-fine was tyrannically operated, and we are inevitably left with the impression that William, while realizing that the Normans who had served him well in war required protection, during the period of transition, from clandestine reprisals, yet felt that his real interest lay in conciliating his new subjects, and welding them with the Normans into one harmonious whole. He did not destroy a unity, but created unity where there had been little before. Those who hailed Harold as the 'last English king of England', and were most vociferous in the battle-cry of 'Harold and Holy Cross', cannot have been greatly disappointed when the help expected from Edwin and Morcar, the earls of Mercia and Northumbria, failed to arrive. They realized that it was due from the friendship of neighbours, rather than from the duty of subjects. Never before 1066 did England enjoy unified government. Canute the Great had dreamed of an Anglo-Danish kingdom spanning the North Sea; William brought to fruition the idea of an Anglo-Norman kingdom of a different shape, an edifice whose base rested in Normandy, while its top storey was bounded on the north by the Tweed, and the Welsh Marches formed its party-wall.

At the time of the Conquest there was no central court. The local courts, of the shires and hundreds, were supreme in their own spheres. The old shire court had nothing in common with the modern county court established by an Act of 1846, whose functions are solely judicial. The old shire court was a kind of local Parliament, and more than a Parliament in the modern sense, for it fulfilled all three of the functions of government, judicial and executive as well as legislative. Its officials were the earl, the bishop, the sheriff, and the suitors. The earl was a kind of local monarch, the repository of temporal, as was the bishop of spiritual power. The suitors were the owners of certain pieces of land who, by virtue of their holding, owed 'suit of court', that is to say, were bound to attend at the shire court, and to act as its judges. Their president was in practice usually the sheriff. The powers of this official were temporarily enhanced as a result of the Norman Conquest, for the earl and bishop ceased to enjoy any predominant position apart from that of mere landowners, and the earls in fact disappeared from most of the shires. The Norman kings saw in the sheriff a useful link between the local administration and themselves, and they made extensive use of him as a royal delegate. But his exaltation proved to be short-lived, for his powers, like those of the shire court, and other courts presided over by him, were rapidly sapped by the expanding authority of the Curia Regis. The hundred court was a lesser court within the shire, presided over by the reeve.

The Norman idea of government was necessarily based on the institution of feudalism. This was not wholly an innovation in England. It was common for a lesser man to put himself and his belongings at the disposal of a greater, in return for protection. And we see the feudal idea implicit in the obligation of suit of court. William gave to that idea articulate and coherent expression. Whereas the Witan was little more than a collection of great men whose advice the king chose to solicit, the Curia Regis, which William put in its place, was composed, partly indeed of some persons specially summoned by him, but chiefly of those who owed their compulsory membership of it to the fact that the king had made grants of land to them, on the understanding that they should perform for him services of various kinds. The word 'tenure' necessarily implies the relation of feudal lord and tenant. It is commonly said that, until the changes in the land law in 1925, there were three kinds of tenure, freehold, copyhold, and leasehold, and that the legislation of that year reduced them to two by abolishing copyhold. But this statement is erroneous, in that leasehold is not a tenure in the strict sense, as it depends, not on the feudal relation, but on a contract between lessor and lessee. The prime division of tenures in the medieval period was into the free tenures, which were of many types, and the unfree, the holding by villeins, who were tied to a piece of land, were bound to perform for their lord agricultural services of an indefinite nature and extent, and could be physically recovered, in case they left the land, by a special writ *de nativo habendo*. Villeins did not become personally free, nor did this writ lose its validity, until the sixteenth century. The old tenure in villeinage became copyhold tenure, so called because it was said to be 'by copy of the court roll', and many peculiar characteristics of the old tenure, logical enough while the villein tenant was unfree, remained attached, as unfortunate anachronisms which gravely complicated the land law, to copyhold lands. The four free tenures were frankalmoign, chivalry, serjeanty,[1] and socage. The obligation of the tenant in frankal-

---

[1] Space does not permit of a detailed description of this tenure. It must be sufficient to say that it was of two varieties, grand and petty; the former approximated to chivalry, the latter to socage.

moign was to pray for the grantor while he lived, and to offer masses for his departed soul. The tenant in chivalry was bound to serve in war, and also to provide a number of armed retainers for the same purpose. This service was generally commuted for a money payment known as scutage. But this exaction was by no means the only, nor the greatest, burden that he had to bear. For he was liable to other pecuniary exactions known as aids and reliefs. Furthermore, the lord had the rights of wardship and marriage. The former entitled him to the custody of the person and lands of the infant heir of his tenant, without any liability to account for profits, while the latter gave him the right to dispose of those heirs in marriage; should a suitable match be refused, its value, assessed by a judge, was forfeited to the lord. Thus it will be seen that on the land law rested not only the general scheme of central government, but also the more specialized and vital system of taxation. The medieval king was expected to 'live of his own', that is to say, to provide for the ordinary expenses of government out of his hereditary revenues, whereof the greater part was formed by the feudal dues. It was only in cases where an extraordinary grant was needed that he must approach Parliament.[2] The tenant in socage enjoyed less dignity, but the incidents of tenure sat far more lightly upon him. His main obligation was to render agricultural services, which were fixed, and not indefinite as were those of the villein. He, like the tenant in chivalry, could compound for these services by a money payment, but whereas the scutage paid by the tenant in chivalry was substantial, the quit rent paid by the socager was nominal. And wardship and marriage, those two most burdensome encombrances of the tenant in chivalry, did not fall on the socager at all. We shall see that the introduction of the system of 'uses' of land tended greatly to decrease the feudal dues coming into the royal coffers, and that Henry VIII temporarily restored the position by the Statute of Uses 1535.[3] But during the first half of the seventeenth century other factors again caused their gradual decrease, and the Act of 1660, which abolished tenures in chivalry and turned them all into socage, rendered the king dependent, for

[2] The king retained, of course, the rents of the Crown lands, which, by 1660, had come to exceed the feudal revenues; but these were quite inadequate to provide for more than the smallest fraction of the expenses of government.

[3] See p. 99.

the ordinary as well as the extraordinary expenses of government, on Parliament.

It has so far been assumed that the person to whom the feudal dues were owed was the king, and it is true that he must be the ultimate and paramount lord of all the land in England. It has been well said of him that he was always lord and never tenant. But his tenants-in-chief had the power of subinfeudation; that is to say, of granting all or part of their land to inferior tenants, to hold of them by feudal tenure, whether free or unfree. But this power was subject to a very important limitation. William, who was himself in Normandy a feudal tenant of the King of France, was much too wise to introduce into England one prominent feature of the system under which he himself held. For in France the military obligation of the inferior tenant bound him to espouse his lord's quarrel even against the king himself. But William was determined to enjoy the best of both worlds; a system which suited him as tenant in France was repugnant to him as King of England, and every inferior military tenant was bound to make a reservation of the overriding duty he owed the king.

It was part and parcel of the position of a feudal lord, that he could hold a court for his tenants. The Curia Regis was essentially the central court that the king, as supreme feudal lord, held for his tenants-in-chief. Likewise we find, parallel with the shire and hundred courts, courts baron and courts customary, which inferior lords held for their free and unfree tenants respectively. The judges in the former were the tenants themselves, who owed suit of court; in the latter the lord's steward was the sole judge.

Henry I took a big step in the direction of cementing the union of Normans and English by marrying a princess who was half-English and half-Scottish, but it was left for his vigorous grandson, Henry II, to do most of the work of spreading the mantle of royal justice, administered in the Curia Regis, over all his subjects. This great king's life work was the centralization of English government and justice. Some of his reforms must be specially noted at this stage, though many others will be unfolded by our subsequent account.

(*a*) He was the pioneer of the system of royal writs, which lies at the root of common law procedure.

(b) He asserted the exclusive jurisdiction of the Curia Regis over all serious crime.

(c) He established the principle of the 'King's Peace'; crime came to be regarded no longer as a wrong against an individual, but rather as a wrong against the State.

(d) He hastened the demise of the older, and unsatisfactory, methods of trial, by developing in part a system of trial by jury.

These four great achievements stand in a very close relation with one another, and must be considered together. Those who have studied Gaius'[4] account of the old *legis actiones* in Roman Law, or the Icelandic *Saga of Burnt Njal*, will not need to be reminded that it is an almost inevitable feature of legal systems in their adolescence that the spirit of the law is overshadowed by the letter of procedure, that the demands of precision far outweigh those of abstract justice. There must arrive a period at which the law appears stagnant, at which a man may approach a tribunal with the burning sense, and the solid fact, of moral wrong, and yet be sent disappointed away, for the sole reason that his case cannot be brought within the orbit of one of the recognized forms of action. The length or brevity of this period provides no unreliable index to the vigour of the social consciousness of the people. In England it can be said that the period of stagnation was short, that the movement, once initiated, towards the full realization of civil justice, though at times slow, was never arrested, until we have at last arrived at the fulfilment of the principle that wherever there is a right, there also should a remedy be found. Maine has told us that the three great agents which have assisted the law to harmonize with the needs of society are legal fictions, equity, and legislation; of each of these three more must be said in its place. But now we are concerned to examine the salient features of civil and criminal procedure which Henry II found when he came to the throne, and the improvements he made. It must be remembered that the preceding reign of Stephen was a troublesome and anarchical time. A state of civil war spells a suspension of progress, and a relapse into the abuses of the past. Much of the beneficial work of Henry I was undone; royal justice languished, and sheriffs forgot that they were servants of the

---

[4] A jurist of the second century A.D. His *Institutes* formed the basis for the *Institutes* of the Emperor Justinian, four hundred years later.

Crown, remembering only their positions of local authority. Cases which should have been referred to the king and his court were disposed of in the shire court and sheriff's tourn by sheriffs who argued, not without reason, that invocations of the king's courts wore an unreal air in the absence of certainty as to the identity of the king. Likewise feudal lords used and abused their powers, and executed justice or injustice in their feudal courts, according to their free will and pleasure. In 1154 the whole land, weary of turmoil and internal strife, hailed as a beacon of hope the accession of that great and strange being, at once so calculating and so passionate, so cautious and so precipitate, so English and so un-English, destined in thirty-five years to lay the sure foundations of English liberty, to play the first sinister act in the tragedy of Anglo-Irish relations, to murder Becket, and to die at last friendless and disappointed, in loneliness and anguish, Henry II.

Let us consider what cases came before the courts at that time. The boundaries between criminal and civil law were not so clearly demarcated as they afterwards became. Crime was looked on as a wrong against an individual, to be atoned for, in blood or in money, according to his choice. The action of trespass, which, with its teeming offspring, was destined to play so big a part in the development of the common law, was not yet born. Trespass was then the name given to the lesser types of crime, later known as misdemeanours.[5] The institution of trial by jury was still in its infancy; the older methods of trial, by compurgation, battle, and ordeal, still held the field. Centuries of use have so familiarized us with the system of indictment for crime at the suit of the State that the revelation, in the case of *Ashford* v. *Thornton* in 1818, that an older method still existed, took the legal profession by surprise. This older method was by 'appeal', at the suit of a private accuser. The issue was tried by battle, or occasionally by ordeal of fire or water. That neither of these methods of trial could possibly supply any reliable indication of the guilt or innocence of the accused, that both held the door wide open to every kind of chicanery, appears so obvious to us now, that we can understand their longevity only by appreciating that it was due, not to love of pageantry, but to a

---

[5] A classification of crimes which was abolished by the Criminal Law Act 1967.

simple and unsophisticated faith. Primitive society was tenacious of the idea that solemn issues cannot safely be referred to the fallible judgement of men, but must be trustfully left to the revelation of God. The chastity of Hermione was determined by the Delphic oracle, the legitimacy of King Hakon the Great of Norway by his mother, Inga of Varteig, undergoing the ordeal of the hot iron. Henry was in advance of his age in realizing that it is unsound, in theology as in common sense, that it is in fact impious, to suppose that God will automatically respond to human interrogation; that the older methods of trial were in fact the product not of religion, but of superstition; that they were in every way inferior to the newer method of trial by jury.

Of belongings which went to make up a man's property, land was, and for five centuries remained, by far the most important, and we are not surprised to learn that the action which loomed largest was the action for the recovery of land. Now technically no subject could own land; it was of the essence of the feudal system that all land was held ultimately of the king, the universal and paramount lord of the land. The subject of dispute must therefore always be, as to which of two claimants was entitled to hold a piece of land of a particular lord. If that lord were himself a subject, the case would be decided in the court baron, where the standard of justice would vary according to the intellectual and moral quality of the tenants who, as we have seen, formed its judges. If, however, the litigants were tenants-in-chief of the king, the case must be tried in the Curia Regis, and was initiated by the writ of right. In both cases the actual method of trying the issue would be by battle. Henry was determined that no man should be compelled to answer for his freehold without the king's writ. That is to say, if one man wished to challenge the title of another to a piece of freehold land, he must invariably first obtain from the Chancellor the writ of right. Of that writ there were two main forms, according as the lord of whom the land was allegedly held were the king or an intermediate lord. If the former, the writ was known as the *Praecipe in capite*; it was issued to the sheriff, and directed him, as a royal delegate, to bring the case before the Curia Regis. If the latter, the writ of right patent was the proper form; it directed the lord to do justice between the parties in his own court, but contained a significant sting in its tail, in a threat that 'if you fail to do justice, then my sheriff will'. Henry did not always wait to give the court baron the chance to do justice, but would by-pass it altogether, by using the *Praecipe in capite* when the writ of right patent was appropriate.

But Henry's programme had far more ambitious aims than the mere establishment of the writ of right as the necessary preliminary to land litigation. He intended to abolish trial by battle, or at any rate to sap its vitality by providing a better alternative. By some enactment lost to us, of which the most probable date is 1179, he instituted the Grand Assize, whereby the tenant against whom a writ of right was brought could avoid trial by battle, and place his case upon the verdict of recognitors.

But why should not the claimant, secure in the consciousness of his own right, short-circuit the leisurely, technical, and laborious process of the writ of right, and simply enter on the land and eject the usurper? Here we meet that maxim which is so sadly maltreated by non-lawyers, 'possession is nine points of the law'. A rational system of law has always two pressing reasons for protecting possession. Firstly, to allow a man to take the law into his own hands, in the assertion of a fancied, or even of a genuine, claim of right, is to invite private violence. Secondly, while ownership is a right, possession is primarily a fact, though attended with considerable legal incidents which distinguish it from mere detention or occupancy. It is, therefore, far more easy to prove the practical fact of possession than the mystical right of ownership. One of the most important principles of the English law of property is that the man in possession is presumed to be owner, unless and until someone else can establish a better title by legal process. Henry ensured that the only effect of precipitate action by a claimant should be the delay of the fulfilment of his claim, and the increase of its cost; for by his institution of the assize of novel disseisin, he provided that an ejected possessor who made prompt application should have a jury empanelled to answer the simple question 'Has A unjustly and without judgement disseised B?' The members of the assize were in no way concerned with the title to the land; but if they answered the question in the affirmative, B must be put back into seisin, and A, having learned the lesson of patience, could then do what he ought to have done at first, and bring the writ of right. The words 'seisin' and 'disseised' demand a note of explanation. The modern student of Greek recognizes the existence, though he may fail to comprehend the utility, in that great language, of three voices, active, passive, and middle. Likewise the modern student of real property law has to learn that medieval law knew of a third relation between a man and land. This relation was seisin, whose importance in modern times has all but vanished. But it played a big part in the history of the land law. It does not form a third parallel between ownership and possession, but runs a zigzag course, inclining now to this side and now to that. It is not necessary here to enter into any part of the intricate learning that it has inspired; it must be sufficient to say that in the time of Henry II it was, to all intents and purposes, synonymous with possession, and so 'disseised' meant simply 'put out of possession'. Later the conception of seisin approximated more closely to that of ownership. Later, too, the assize of novel disseisin, which wears, to modern eyes, inevitably the air of a temporary expedient, disappeared under the gradual supremacy of a new theory that a person entitled to land has normally a right of entry on it. His entry, however, had to be peaceful, for by a statute of Richard II in 1381, which was not repealed until 1977, forcible entry was made criminal.

Supposing, however, that a feudal lord, on the death of a tenant, refused to admit his heir in his place? For this precise case the Assize of Northampton, 1176, introduced the assize of mort d'ancestor, whereby a jury was empanelled to answer the following questions: (1) Did A, the father (mother, brother, sister, uncle, or aunt) of the claimant, die seised of the land? (2) Did A die within the time prescribed for bringing the action? (3) Is the claimant A's next heir? If all these questions were answered in the affirmative, the claimant was put into seisin.

These assizes were two of the constellation of three which legal history knows under the name of the possessory assizes. It is convenient here to mention the third, the assize of darrein presentment, whose function was to discover the identity of the patron who last presented an incumbent to a particular church.

The fundamental division of property in English Law is not, as in Roman Law, the natural division into moveables and immoveables, but an artificial, and far more difficult, division into real and personal property. These adjectives would be classified by grammarians as 'transferred epithets'. For it was very early established that it was not in all actions that success would be attended by the specific recovery of the property. Only the writ of right, for the recovery of freehold land, would have this effect; the ambition of actions concerning chattels was bounded by the aim of compelling the payment of damages. Actions for the specific recovery of property were known as real actions, the rest as personal actions. So types of property specifically recoverable came to be known as real property, while other types were brought under the heading of personal property. The division did not coincide with the natural division into moveables and immoveables, for while title-deeds relating to freehold land could be specifically recovered, leasehold land, the nature of which must be fully discussed later, could not, and so ranked as personal property. The mere artificiality of the division would have been harmless had it been recognized; but the law took the division seriously, and made it a matter of substance, by establishing a dual system of intestate succession. Prior to the long overdue changes of 1925, if a man had a son and two daughters, and died intestate, leaving a leasehold house, surrounded by a freehold garden and parkland, the son would succeed to the garden and park to the entire exclusion of his sisters, but the house would be divided between all three children. The questions are often asked, how far did the legislation of 1925 assimilate the law of real and personal property, and would a complete assimilation be possible or desirable? The simple answer is that the true assimilation has been that of the artificial English division into real and personal property with the Roman and Continental division into moveables and immoveables, which is inherent in the very nature of things. For while nothing is legally impossible to Parliament, it is physically impossible for any human agency to tamper with the essential indestructibility of land, and so, while the laws of succession on intestacy to all kinds of property have become virtually unified, the rule that land cannot be stolen is, in effect, no more susceptible of legal alteration than are the proper seasons for the growth of vegetables.

In the time of Henry II, the twin laws of tort and contract were but beginning to stir in the womb of the criminal law. Their delivery was destined to take place during the reign of Henry III, through the services of the action of trespass, which has been so aptly described by Maitland as the 'fertile mother of actions'. The designation of trespass would then shift to civil from criminal law, to which it was anchored at the period we are now considering. But there were older personal actions which had even then established their identity. The action of debt lay for the recovery of money owed, the action of detinue for the recovery of damages for the detention by the defendant of the plaintiff's chattel. The method of trial in both these actions was compurgation, or wager of law, which appears to us as more haphazard and unsatisfactory than battle, or even than ordeal. If the defendant could get twelve 'compurgators' to swear to the truth of his denial, their oath was final, and its veracity could not be questioned. If, however, they did not swear in the proper form, 'the oath burst', and the defendant would lose his case.

Let us return to criminal law. To change laws, to improve a system—these are within the reach of industrious mediocrity; but the eradication of pernicious ideas, and their replacement by a sound philosophy of government, are possible only to genius. Henry II had genius of a high order, which never manifested itself more clearly than in his appreciation of the inevitability of the divergence of the paths of crime and of tort, and in his conception of crimes as offences against the whole community, as 'pleas of the Crown'. It was characteristic of his restless and dynamic energy that hot on the heels of diagnosis followed treatment. His plan, as revealed in the Assize of Clarendon, 1166, and the Assize of Northampton, 1176, had no less an ambition than the complete centralization of criminal justice in the Curia Regis. But it was no part of Henry's plan that all pleas of the Crown should be heard before the full court. Centralization of control, not of administration, was his aim. R. C. K. Ensor, in his admirable monograph on *Courts and Judges*, made the generalization that the tendency of English practice has been towards central administration of civil, and local administration of criminal, justice. Henry adopted and perfected the system of travelling commissioners, or itinerant justices, which had been employed by William I for the conduct of local inquiries on which was based the great land survey known as Domesday Book. Having got it working on oiled wheels, he adapted it to two vital ends, the supervision of local government, and the local trial, by royal justices, of pleas of the Crown. The former function was discharged by the General Eyre, whose justices are the ancestors of the district auditors of the present day, and the latter by the commissioners of assize, whose circuits pursued an uninterrupted course from the time of Henry II until 1971.

Henry fostered and encouraged the new method of criminal procedure by indictment, or accusation at the suit of the State, which necessarily involved trial by jury. But he was too wise to attempt the sudden extinction of the old system of appeal at the suit of a private accuser. He realized to the full that the sentiment of a people cannot be forced, that it must be left to itself to catch up with the foresight of a statesman. He was content to purge the appeal of its abuses, and to allow it to continue side by side with the indictment. Shakespeare, in words put into the mouth of Richard II, reminds us that the appeal was often brought for improper motives. The king, having asked John of Gaunt whether he has brought with him his son Henry Bolingbroke, 'to make good the boisterous late *appeal* against the Duke of Norfolk, Thomas Mowbray', continues:

> Tell me, moreover, hast thou sounded him
> If he appeal the duke on ancient malice,
> Or worthily, as a good subject should,
> On some known ground of treachery in him?

Shakespeare must have had in mind the writ *de odio et atia*, invented by Henry II. It enabled a person appealed to submit to the verdict of recognitors the question whether he had been appealed through hatred and malice. The effect of an affirmative finding would be to destroy the appeal, and thus the trial by battle could not proceed.

No appreciation of the legislative achievements of Henry II would be complete without some reference to the Assize of Arms 1181. Cutting right across any feudal relation, there was a duty, incumbent on every free man, to serve in war. By this enactment Henry II regulated and standardized the duty, establishing a scale of weapons, based on his wealth, which each man must provide.

3 The thirteenth century

Had Edward the Confessor devoted himself to the practice of efficient government as well as to that of holy life, had longer time been given to Harold before the flood of invasion burst upon him, had that invasion been from one quarter only, and not from east and south simultaneously, the victory of royal over local government and justice might have been effected at an earlier date. As things turned out, it was left to Henry II to decide for all succeeding ages the unitary character of the English Constitution. With his work vanished forever any possibility that it might develop on federal lines. He goes down to history as the great centralizer. But he did not differentiate and allocate the functions of government. The movement towards the separation of legislative, executive, and judicial powers, though never at any time completed, was inaugurated by his great-grandson, Edward I. Henry II built the walls of the Curia Regis with imperishable stone; Edward I, while preserving and strengthening its fabric, began to let out the building in flats. In his reign we find a definite distribution of common law jurisdiction between three courts: Common Pleas,[1] for the trial of disputes between subject and subject; King's Bench, for pleas of the Crown; Exchequer, for revenue matters.[2]

In 1187 the Curia Regis towered supreme over its rivals. These fell into three groups: the sheriff's courts, the feudal courts, and the franchise courts. The sheriff's courts were the *shire court* for both civil and criminal matters, and the *sheriff's tourn* for petty crime only. It was not until after the Statute of Gloucester in 1278 that the actual jurisdiction of the shire court was seriously abridged. That Statute provided that no action should be brought in the

[1] We shall see that Common Pleas may be said to have begun its career as a separate court under Henry II; p. 35.
[2] The Exchequer as an administrative department of finance existed as early as the reign of Henry I.

Curia Regis if the amount at stake were less than forty shillings. It was really aimed at preventing congestion in the Curia Regis, but it was interpreted in the reverse sense, as limiting the shire court to cases in which the amount at stake fell below forty shillings. But it must be remembered that the sheriff was not only the chief man in a county; he was also an important royal deputy, and Henry II found him, through his courts, a useful watchdog of royal interests, their safeguard against the feudal courts. We have touched on his ingenious method of using the threat of intervention by the sheriff in order to ensure obedience by a lord to a writ of right patent. Further, the sheriff was furnished with the writ of *tolt*, whereby he could take the initiative, and remove a case from a feudal court into the shire court. Again, the writ of *justicies* opened up to him a large potential field of activity, for it could give him unlimited jurisdiction in any circumstances. But this writ in practice became obsolete, and the writ of tolt died a natural death with the supersession of both forms of writ of right by the newer action of ejectment, which must be fully discussed at a later stage. But though Henry was prepared to bolster up the shire court, if he could use it as an aid to royal justice, he had no idea of keeping alive its jurisdiction for its own sake. He would, whenever it served his purpose, remove a case into the Curia Regis from the shire court by the writ of *pone*. Its jurisdiction, too, must have tended automatically to decrease as a result of Henry's institution of a new central court of law, which was the forerunner of the Court of Common Pleas. Of the sheriff's tourn it need only be repeated that the effect of the Assizes of Clarendon and Northampton was to limit its jurisdiction to petty offences, and to remark that sometimes a tourn got into private hands through royal grant, when it was known as a *court leet*, a name which it shared with other courts of special jurisdiction.

The feudal courts must be distinguished from the franchise courts. The former emerged as a natural projection of the principle that it is an indispensable function of feudal lordship to hold a court for the tenants. We have seen how Henry exerted a check on feudal courts by ensuring that no man be put to answer for his freehold without the king's writ, and by the use of the writ of tolt. But the franchise jurisdictions owe their origin to special royal grants. They were of many varieties. Sometimes a franchise would be granted to a great landowner, quite apart from his status as a feudal lord; an example of this type survived in the shape of the Chancery Court of the County Palatine of Lancaster until it was abolished by the Courts Act 1971. Others were granted to professional interests; thus the Courts of the Chancellors of Oxford and Cambridge Universities, also only recently abolished. To yet others may be traced the beginnings of the medieval Law Merchant, which merits fuller discussion later.

In our journey from the modern constitution back to the age of Henry II, we must forget the familiar landmarks of our starting-point. The very existence of a bicameral legislature, of which the Upper House should include an hereditary membership, while the Lower should be composed of the elected representatives of the people, on which the king should be dependent for money, to which his ministers should be responsible, and from which his judges should be excluded, still lay at some distance in the future. Membership of the Curia Regis belonged to the king's tenants-in-chief, whether lay or clerical. Their ranks were swollen by the attendance of other persons whom the king specially summoned as advisers. It presented the aspect of a united, conglomerate body, composed of two classes, whom Holdsworth calls the magnates and the curiales. It operated, within itself, all three organs of government. It passed laws, it performed the routine of administration, and it adjudicated on disputes, whether public or private. To attribute to Henry II any idea of separating the three functions is unthinkable; as well might one suggest that Wycliffe envisaged Tractarianism, or Newton aeroplanes. That the constitution gradually orientated itself in the direction of the doctrine of the separation of powers was due to the accession of a bad king, whose misgovernment had the effect of driving a wedge between the magnates and the curiales, and uniting the former in firm alliance with the English people.

At one time it was the fashion to 'debunk' previously accepted historical conceptions. This process usually took the form of puncturing the reputations of characters whose integrity had been regarded as unimpeachable. Now the tide appears to be setting in the opposite direction. Attempts have been made to dispel the fog of prejudice which has enshrouded Pope Alexander VI and Catherine de Medici, while Josephine Tey, in her novel *The Daughter of Time* (1951), is now widely regarded as having made an unanswerable defence of Richard III against the calumnies heaped upon him in past centuries, and perpetuated by Shakespeare's great play. Bishop Stubbs pointed out that nobody had been found to say a good word for King John, and yet Dr. Richardson and Professor Sayles, in *The Governance of Mediaeval England* (1963), have shown that John had at least an arguable case in the great issues of his reign. He may have been to some extent false, cowardly, and tyrannical, yet these vices, combined with his military failures abroad, brought about that very consummation which William I had envisaged, and Henry I and Henry II had laboured to achieve, the union of Normans and English into one nation. The events of his reign brought his subjects to the earliest realization of that truth which, though periodically forgotten, has always returned to their minds with reinforced strength, that the secret of England's power and virtue lies in her insular geographical position. John of Gaunt could never have truly called her 'this precious stone set in the silver sea', had not the loss of Normandy by his ancestor and namesake enshrined her in her island home.

The barons, in forcing John to issue Magna Carta in 1215, were acting in no sectional or partisan spirit, but from a high sense of the common good of all, and as the spokesmen of the nation. They were too wise and honest to have failed to recognize the immense value of Henry II's reforms. Thus, much of Magna Carta is in essence a restatement of the work of that great king, which had been in many cases blurred and blotted by his unworthy, though favourite son. But they were still barons, and with all their honesty and singleness of heart, they could not be expected to cast aside all care for the interests of their own order. In the Charter, therefore, two voices speak: side by side with clauses which breathe the spirit of benevolent reform, we find others which rebuild the rampart round baronial privilege. But the destiny of events willed it that the reactionary clauses, though never repealed, should perish from inanition, while the progressive clauses should remain the model of all future legislative development. Thus we have seen that Henry II was over-eager in asserting his control over litigation affecting land; that he sometimes issued the writ *Praecipe in capite* when he ought to have issued the writ of right patent, thus causing the lord 'to lose his court'. By the 34th clause this practice was checked. Now this clause was never formally repealed: Henry II's abuse was never legalized; but all the same the clause soon lost all its effect, for the writ of right was itself largely superseded by the newer action of ejectment, though it lived on as an uneasy ghost which made intermittent appearances until, along with other real actions, it was finally exorcized by the Real Property Limitation Act 1833.

The famous 39th clause has been much misunderstood. It lays down, in effect, that no free man shall undergo imprisonment or loss, otherwise than by the judgment of his peers and/or by the law of the land. Now the latter of these two requrements has been rightly hailed as a legislative declaration of the rule of law, as a harbinger of the 'due process of law' without which, according to the Fifth and Fourteenth Amendments to the American Constitution, nobody can be deprived of life, liberty, or property. But it has now been abundantly shown that much of the enthusiasm shown for the former requirement was misplaced, that it referred, not to trial by jury, but to the trial of a peer by the body of his peers for treason or felony. Thus the clause, which was popularly supposed to be the generous fountain of English liberty and equality before the law, was, in reality, redolent of feudal privilege; and the privilege belonged, not to the individual peer, but to the order of peerage, and so it could not be waived, no other court having jurisdiction in the case. The privilege was abolished by the Criminal Justice Act 1948, which places peers, for the purposes of criminal law, on the same footing as commoners.

But for one clause which restores feudal privilege we can point to five which give progressive effect to Henry II's system. John had allowed sheriffs to arrogate to themselves once more the power of hearing pleas of the Crown; the 24th clause placed such cases, once and for all, outside the jurisdiction of sheriffs, and restricted them to the trial of petty offences in the tourn; their sole duty, in the case of more serious crime, was to secure the arrest of the offenders, and their appearance before the itinerant justices. Under John the dread snakeling of venal justice had reared its ugly head; Magna Carta thrust it back for ever into the abyss whence it came, not only by the 36th clause, which concerned especially the writ *de odio et atia*, but also by the comprehensive 40th clause, which writes in imperishable letters the noble principle that 'right and justice shall not be sold or denied or delayed'.

By enforcing on John the issue of the Charter, the barons attained the full extent of their object. The republican sentiments of Thackeray's character, 'Lord Magnus Charters, the Marquis of Runnymede's son', would have found no echo in the breast of his thirteenth-century ancestor. The barons never dreamed of deposing the king; on the contrary, he must remain and rule well. But never again should he or his chosen advisers be allowed to flout the rights of his subjects, great or small. On this were all, whether Norman earls or Saxon churls, inexorably determined. Thenceforth the magnates stood aloof, passing in stern review the conduct of the king and his advisers, unsparing alike in approval of good government and in frustration of bad. The chariot of the constitution had begun to move on the first stage of its journey towards that goal which it has never reached, but which the framers of the American Constitution attained at one bound, the doctrine of the separation of powers. In America the three organs of government resemble three flowers in one bed; in England they resemble rather three flowers on one stalk.

We must now examine the gradual differentiation and allocation of functions. The process had actually been begun by Henry II himself. The monk of Peterborough, the historian of his reign, has given an account of his establishment, in 1178, of a body of five judges, to be a supreme tribunal on all legal questions, with an appeal to himself and such members of the Curia Regis as he cared to call into consultation. This court, which is the parent of the Court of Common Pleas, had no functions other than judicial, and so was a 'court' in the full modern sense of the term. Clause 17 of Magna Carta afforded statutory recognition to the court by providing that it should not follow the king in his progresses, but remain fixed at one place, which afterwards was named as Westminster.

But the main point of cleavage was between the curiales and the magnates. The events of the reign of John, and their culmination at Runnymede, had helped to breed an atmosphere of suspicion, and a realization of diversity of interest, between these two classes. Within the Curia Regis appear two bodies fulfilling different functions. The legislative office remained with the main body of the Curia Regis, the magnates, who were to be joined fifty years later by the elected representatives of the people, while the executive office fell to the curiales, who remained permanently at the side of the king.

We are, of course, still far removed from the modern principle that the ministers of the Crown are responsible to Parliament. This result could never be achieved until the king's finances became wholly dependent on Parliamentary grant; and until the abolition of military tenures in 1660 his feudal dues kept him independent of Parliament, which he need summon only if he required an extraordinary sum for some special purpose. But Magna Carta, though acquiescing entirely in the perpetuation of the legitimate feudal revenues, is careful to prevent the king from making arbitrary additions to them. By the 12th clause it is laid down that the king shall not levy any extraordinary aids or scutages 'unless by the common counsel of the Realm'. But in our study of this clause we must not make the fatal mistake of anticipating the course of history. The clause in no way foreshadowed the principle, which has only in very modern times been fully established, that taxation depends on representation. For it is followed up by clause 14, which enumerates those whose counsel is to be sought, and we search in vain for any element akin to the modern House of Commons. It was not until the reign of Henry III that the representative idea rose into the ascendant, and the first Parliament which heralded in any real sense the bicameral legislature of the present day was that called by Simon de Montfort in 1265. The assembly contemplated by the Charter was, in short, more like a House of Lords without a House of Commons, and the clause leaves a loophole which enables the king to treat some, and some only, of those entitled to be summoned, as necessary parties to legislation and taxation. Thus the door is opened to a duplication, a rivalry of legislative power, an enactment which is the creature of King, Lords, and Commons, being known as a Statute, as distinguished from an Ordinance, issued by the king after consultation with some body of advisers which might with some show of justice be said to satisfy the provisions of clauses 12 and 14.

When John died, his son, Henry III, 'the cygnet to this pale faint swan', was but a child. During his reign great events occurred, and it was a reign which looms large in the formation of the constitution, the age which Maitland has aptly called 'the golden age of English case-law'. On the complex character of the king himself Sir

Maurice Powicke has shed an interesting light. He had ability, but it was marred by restlessness and petulance. He was not without some qualities of statesmanship, but he was a man of activity rather than of action, not, in fine, really a strong man. Our wonder that he should have been the son of the vicious and vacillating John is exceeded only by our amazement that he should have been the father of the resolute and dominating Edward I. But as the reign of the weak Hezekiah was immortalized by the statecraft and prophecies of Isaiah, so was that of Henry III made memorable by the work of one of England's greatest jurists. The name by which we know him, Bracton, is one that no man coveting the title of lawyer can ignore. All arguments concerning the nature and scope of the royal prerogative must of necessity take as their starting-point his famous aphorism that 'the King is below no man, but he is below God and the law; the King is bound to obey the law, though if he breaks it his punishment must be left to God'. But the chief interest of Bracton lies in his exposition of private, rather than in his speculations as to public, law. His great work *De Legibus et Consuetudinibus Angliae* is, properly speaking, two treatises in one. Of him, as of few others, can that hackneyed phrase 'the parting of the ways' be truly employed. One way led back, through the populous labyrinth of the Glossators' learning, to Justinian's highly developed code of Roman Law, the other pointed forward to the virgin soil of the English common law. Which was to prevail? Was England to follow the course which Scotland at a later period enthusiastically adopted, and yield to the influence of Roman Law in her own system? Or was she to follow the bent of her own philosophy, and carve out a new system, based on the royal writs? When Bracton died, the answer to this question rested still in suspense, but during the reign of Edward I the scales were finally tipped on the side of the common law. The role of Roman Law became relegated to the provision of analogies, not of precedents.

Edward I has been called 'the English Justinian'. No appellation could be more inapposite. Justinian stood at the end of a process, Edward at an early stage of its course. The Roman world of the sixth century was surfeited with legal authority, that of thirteenth-century England starved for the lack of it. Hence Justinian was a codifier, Edward a pioneer. His reign saw the passage of much legislation, in the fields both of public and of private law.

By the Statute Quia Emptores 1290 he effectively increased the importance of his own feudal position at the expense of that of all inferior lords. It is impossible to understand the Statute without forming an accurate appreciation of the position of the freehold tenant of land. It is interesting to recall to memory the Sankey Coal Commission of 1919. The policy of nationalization,[3] which the Commission ultimately recommended, was urged by some of the miners' representatives on another ground than that of mere policy. They took their stand upon a view of the land law which enabled them to regard the confiscatory measure of their desire, in the light, not of a change of that law, but of a rescue of that law from an abuse which disfigured it. The argument was as follows: no subject can hold land, but the king is the only true and ultimate landowner; in these days the king, as chief executive, is identified with the State; a Nationalization Act, therefore, would simply be an assertion and vindication of a State ownership which already existed. But the fallacy of this argument can be expressed in the one word 'tenure'. Admittedly none of the coalowners legally owned their land, but they held it, as successors in title of those to whom the Conqueror had originally granted it. Once such a grant had been made, it could not be recalled. The king could, in case of failure on the part of the tenant to perform his feudal services, levy distress upon the land. But he could get the land into his own hands again only in one of two ways, by forfeiture, in case of the conviction of the tenant for treason, or by escheat, in case the tenant were convicted of felony, or died intestate without heirs. The word 'heirs' demands an explanation, for there is no word which non-lawyers have more cruelly misused. The heir had nothing to do with a will. He was[4] simply the person designated by law to succeed to land on the intestacy of the tenant. His claims could, therefore, be overridden by an alienation of the land by the tenant in his lifetime, or by the terms of his will, provided that such courses were legally open to him.[5] In early times they were not.

---

[3] This was eventually carried into effect, by the Coal Industry Nationalization Act 1946.

[4] He is referred to here in the past tense, as the effect of certain provisions of the Property legislation of 1925, which need not be described in a book of a general character, has been virtually to abolish him. See Geldart, *Elements of English Law*, 8th ed., pp. 121–125.

[5] See p. 98.

The Conqueror did not broadcast gifts of land blindly. He exercised a wise discrimination in his choice of tenants. It was no part of his policy that a tenant should have the power of allowing the land to pass out of his family into the hands of a stranger who might, from the king's point of view, be an unsatisfactory substitute. But tenants soon acquired the right of alienation in their lifetime, though not, until much later, that of testation. The alienation, from the feudal aspect, would take one of two forms. It might be by subinfeudation or by substitution. By the former method, a lord, who held of another lord, or of the king, would in turn grant a piece of land to a tenant to be held of him. But the latter method would involve his own elimination from the alienated land, and his replacement by the alienee, as tenant of his immediate overlord. The Statute Quia Emptores did two things: it acknowledged the right of free alienation in their lifetime by tenants other than the king's tenants in chief;[6] but stipulated that it should always be by way of substitution and not of subinfeudation. It thus effectually prevented any increase in the number of freehold tenants of an inferior lord, and greatly reduced the work of the feudal courts. Whenever we find a freehold tenant holding land of any lord other than the king, we know that the grant of the land to his predecessor in title by his lord's predecessor must have taken effect before 1290.

The tenant of land with a full right of alienation, otherwise than on his death, was known as the tenant in fee simple. His position differed hardly at all in practice from that of a true owner. But by the Statute *de donis conditionalibus* in 1285, which formed part of the Statute of Westminster II, Edward established the system of entailing land, that is to say, ensuring that, by the use of words restricting the succession to the heirs of the body of the grantee, the land should remain in the family of the grantee unless and until the heirs became extinct, and on such an event should return to the grantor. The elaborate fortress of the unbarrable entail was gradually undermined by those indefatigable burrowing moles, the medieval conveyancers, whose interests lay all in the direction of the easy alienation of land; but it still remains the foundation of the modern 'settlement'.

In another part of the same statute we find the famous clause

---

[6] They acquired the right under a statute of Edward III.

which established the writs *in consimili casu*. To understand these, which have played a very large part in the development of the common law, we must revert to the work of the courts, and see how far it has progressed since the time of Henry II. We have already touched on the writ of right, for the recovery of land, and those of debt and detinue, brought respectively for the recovery of money owed, and damages for the detention of a chattel. To these should be added covenant and account. The field covered by the latter was comparatively narrow, though it is especially interesting in that it formed one of the main bridges between common law and equity. The parties to the action must necessarily stand in a confidential relationship to one another; Ames described its general purpose thus: 'One who received money from another to be applied in a particular way was bound to give an account of his stewardship'; and the conception of stewardship formed, as we shall see, the main plank of the duty of a feoffee to uses of land.[7] In order to understand the action of covenant, it is instructive to compare the English with the Roman idea of contract. The first thing that a student passing from the study of the latter to that of the former must notice is the absence in English Law of that precise classification of contracts into real, verbal, literal, and consensual, with which he has been familiarized by his perusal of the Institutes. The Roman standpoint was that no agreement was entitled to rank as an enforceable contract unless it could present certain credentials; or, to put the matter as it is put by an anonymous medieval rhymester, a pact requires clothing to hide its nakedness. This clothing is supplied, in the case of real contracts, by delivery of money or of a chattel; in the case of verbal and literal contracts, by set forms of speech or of writing; in the case of the consensual contracts of sale, hire, partnership, and agency, by *causa civilis*, which may be roughly interpreted as commercial importance. Other agreements later won their way into the charmed circle, which thus became less and less exclusive, but at no time in the history of Roman Law was admission granted indifferently to all comers. Far different was the course taken by contract in English Law. No writer of a textbook on the subject would dream of arranging his material so as to devote one chapter to sale of goods,

[7] See p. 98.

another to hire-purchase, a third to insurance, and so on. For though there are many differences between these three contracts, they are differences of detail only, for all are equally valid, and enforceable by the courts, provided that they satisfy certain fundamental requirements, which later discussion will reveal. The position ultimately reached by English Law is the antithesis of the Roman doctrine, for in England every agreement is an enforceable contract unless there is some reason why it should be denied this designation.

But it was not until some three centuries after the time of Edward I that this development fully worked itself out; his era was that of Bracton, who clapsed with his right hand the mature and sedate genius of Roman Law, and with his left the buoyant and untried spirit of English common law. The juxtaposition of the two was still sufficiently close for the former to exert over the latter an influence which, though it has waned through the centuries, has never suffered total eclipse. It is not surprising that the circumference of English contract was originally narrower than that of contract in Roman Law. The field of the real contract was covered by the actions of debt and detinue, but the consensual contract was nowhere. Contemporary legal opinion, whether conscious or unconscious, was that if parties cared sufficiently about an agreement to regard it as a suitable matter for litigation, they must take the trouble to embody it in a set and solemn form. The form peculiar to English Law was the seal, and for the enforcement of a contract under seal lay the action of covenant, which thus performed for English Law the function performed for Roman Law by actions proper to verbal and literal contracts. It was not until a considerably later period that the tight circle expanded, but when that time came, it did not stop, as was the case in Roman Law, at the enlargement of its circumference, but burst like a bubble, with the admission of all and every type of agreement through the operation of one of the vigorous offspring of the action of trespass, assumpsit.

It is convenient here for the first time to mention, what must be repeatedly stressed hereafter, that the growth of assumpsit, as of all derivatives of trespass, was much helped on by the desire of the Court of King's Bench to extend its jurisdiction, to which trespass must, as a plea of the Crown, properly belong, at the expense of that of the Common Pleas, which naturally embraced the real actions, and the older personal actions of debt, detinue, covenant, and account. The separation of these two common law courts, and of the Court of Exchequer, from the main body of the Curia Regis, is part of the great work of differentiation of functions, which supplied the complement to the centralizing activity of Henry II, and which Edward I set on its way. Sir Matthew Hale, the great judge and writer of the seventeenth century, has summarized Edward's contribution to constitutional development in terms to which nothing need be added: 'he did much to settle and establish the distributive justice of the kingdom'. Discussion of the important writs *in consimili casu* must wait until we have, in the next chapter, further examined the state of English government in the time of the greatest of all the Plantagenets.

4 Edward I and after

A man standing on a high hill can command a view over the
countryside, and can clearly distinguish fields, lakes, and woods,
each in their own areas. But a traveller through the woods, though
hoping to reach the hill-top through the fields and along the line of
the lakes, has perhaps in the most toilsome part of his journey no
exact idea of the locality of those fields and lakes. Yet he has
necessarily a knowledge of the immediate difficulties besetting him
which escape the eye of the man on the hill-top, whose view cannot
but be imperfect. A modern historian of the period covered by the
twelfth and thirteenth centuries is a very distant observer, and he
must guard against the fatal lure of over-simplification. To assert
baldly that Henry II was the great centralizer, Edward I the great
differentiator of functions, is to make a rather misleading general
statement. History does not lightly yield up her secrets, nor even
when revealed do they cease to bewilder. To indicate the paths
along which the legislative, executive, and judicial functions
diverged is a matter of great complexity. For the process was not
constant; each child of the parent body took with it some of the toys
belonging to the others, and at many points reunions took place
and toys were exchanged. What place in constitutional history are
we to allot to Edward I? The view of Stubbs was that he conscious-
ly, and of set policy, inaugurated the principle of representative
government, by calling to his Model Parliament, along with the
feudal magnates, clerical and lay, and the judges, the elected
representatives of the people, the knights of the shires and the
burgesses of the boroughs. Now Edward I was indeed a man of
vision, and it is true that in the history of the legislature his Model
Parliament of 1295 must demand very close attention, but to
attribute to him the motive of bringing the Commons gradually to
supremacy in the spheres of legislation and taxation is to paint as
false a picture as that painted by Cymbeline when he traced the

origin of our kingship and our laws to the legendary Mulmutius. It is always tempting to say of one king that he did this, of another that he did that; to attribute to conscious design results which must really have flowed from the trend of a policy. But history moves on a regular course, now vigorously, now sluggishly, rather than in a series of jerks, and its development is shaped by the co-operation of the many, rather than by the achievements of the few.

It was in Edward I's reign that Parliament became more and more conscious of its own power; it was in his reign, again, that the three common law courts split off from the main body of the Curia Regis. But we must avoid the easy and seductive generalization that Edward I deliberately separated the legislative, executive, and judicial powers. The separation, which was never to be more than partial, followed inevitably the tendency of events.

The effect of the misgovernment of John had been to place the magnates in opposition against the curiales, and to force him to issue Magna Carta in vindication, partly of feudal privilege, but very largely also of the fundamental interests of the whole people. The arbitrary government that they had taken from John, they would by no means allow Henry III to regain. But the conflict must not be regarded as one between oligarchic and democratic forces. Rather it was waged between two rival oligarchic circles, one with a narrow, the other with a wider circumference. The suspicion of the former felt by the latter found its vent in the Provisions of Oxford 1258. We must return to the forms of action, which, in a study of our judicial system, can never be far from our minds. At the beginning of Henry III's reign, we find the Curia Regis, on its judicial side, working through the system of royal writs, which owed its vigour, if not its origin, to the policy of Henry II. The writ of right for the recovery of land, the possessory assizes for the protection of possession, debt for the recovery of money owed, detinue for the detention of a chattel, covenant for breach of contract, later to be confined to contracts under seal: these formed the staple diet of the practitioner of the early thirteenth century. Any case falling outside the orbit of these forms of action must go to Parliament, in its capacity—which Professor McIlwain labels as its primary capacity in the Middle Ages—of a supreme court of law. But during the first part of Henry III's reign a new planet swam into the ken of the common law, for the action of trespass broke free from the criminal law and started on its meteoric career, whose climax was reached only when it had, through its greater flexibility and other merits, established complete ascendancy over all other writs. Prior to Henry III's reign, crimes were divided into felonies and trespasses,[1] but then the field of tort began to separate itself from that of crime; the more serious trespasses remained criminal, under the name of misdemeanours, and the less serious segregated themselves altogether from the criminal, and attached themselves to the civil sphere.

The writ of trespass was of three kinds, according as injury was done to (*a*) the person, (*b*) land, (*c*) chattels. In (*a*) the writ was trespass *vi et armis*, in (*b*) it was trespass *quare clausum fregit*, in (*c*) it was trespass *de bonis asportatis*. But its development into these clear forms was gradual. As Professor Milsom has shown, in the thirteenth century trespass meant no more than wrong (as is indeed the meaning of the word in the Lord's Prayer), and it covered not only direct injuries, but also many wrongs of an indirect and non-forcible kind. The writs of trespass were either general, where the wrong alleged amounted to direct interference with the complainant, or special, in which case a special explanation of the reason for an act being wrongful was included in the writ. The general writs were at first developed much more freely than the special writs, which perhaps accounts for the belief held by many scholars till recently that the writ of trespass was itself confined to cases of direct damage. It is characteristic of all early legal systems that a period arrives at which the interests of precision appear to outweigh those of universal redress of wrongs, when formalism counts for everything, and abstract justice for very little. In the mid-thirteenth century, if John's boat was tied up to the shore, and George cut the rope, thereby causing the loss of the boat, all that John could recover by way of damages in trespass would be the value of the rope, as George had not been in physical contact with the boat. But Chancellors showed a progressive spirit in widening the writs to meet cases of indirect damage, and by 1370 the use of the special writs of trespass in the royal courts increased. These ultimately became known as writs of trespass on the case, or simply case.

---

[1] A classification abolished by the Criminal Law Act 1967.

The adolescent Parliament viewed with some suspicion the powers of the Chancellors and their clerks to grant new writs, and the Provisions of Oxford 1258 laid down that Chancellors should not, on their own initiative, introduce procedural innovations to satisfy the needs of particular litigants. Yet even Parliament came to see the advantage of leaving some discretion to officials, and it was soon content to concede to the Chancellor, in the interests of legal progress, the power of framing new writs which he had presumed to take. We have had occasion to mention Edward I's famous Statute of Westminster II, whose chapter *de donis conditionalibus* introduced the entail of land. By another provision, equally famous, it recited that in certain cases a remedy was found, but similar cases were left without remedies, and expressly conferred on the Clerks of the Chancery the power to frame new writs to meet these cases, in order that the resources of the law might be made adequate to the demands of justice. Considerable controversy has raged round these writs *in consimili casu*, and some scholars have thought that a relationship existed between them and the writ of case. But the result of Professor Milsom's researches renders this possibility unlikely.[2]

Edward I, following the precedent set by Simon De Montfort, called to his Parliament not only the magnates, but also knights from the shires and burgesses from the boroughs. Why did he do so? His object was certainly not to make them indispensable parties to legislation. The Statute Quia Emptores 1290 was passed before their arrival. Nor were they allowed to regard their summons as a right. They were called if the king needed them, and not otherwise. Dr. Pasquet, in his illuminating essay on the origins of the House of Commons, attributes two motives to Edward I. The main motive was to bring all his subjects under his immediate authority, levelling distinctions between his tenants-in-chief and their sub-tenants, by the process of bringing all together to the same assembly under his common presidency. This is the policy which is implicit in the Statute Quia Emptores, and inevitably leads towards the supersession of the notion of feudal aids by that of national taxes. It is the same policy which led him to turn on the

---

[2] See the *Law Quarterly Review*, vol. 74, pp. 195, 407, 561 (1958); also Milsom, *Historical Foundations of the Common Law*, chaps. 11 and 12.

various franchise jurisdictions the deadly artillery of his Quo Warranto inquiries. These took the form of a questionnaire, consisting of one sentence of terrible simplicity. Could the person assuming to exercise franchise jurisdiction produce a warrant, in the shape of a Royal Charter, for such exercise? If he failed to satisfy the searching test, he was deprived of his court. At first Edward rigidly applied the theory of Bracton, that no length of user could compensate for the lack of a charter, but later he relented, and by the two Statutes of Gloucester, of 1290, uninterrupted user since 1189 was to suffice to confer a good title. His subsidiary motive was to gain in advance the assent of the moneyed mercantile interests for his imposition of aids, and the promise of their co-operation, and that of the knights of the shires, in their collection.

We are not fully conversant with the difference between a Statute, enacted by King, Lords, and Commons, which is universally binding, and an Ordinance or Proclamation, enunciated by King in Council, which is devoid of effect unless (*a*) it is in the sphere of foreign affairs, wherein the Crown is supreme so long as no change in the law of England is involved, or (*b*) the power of legislation has expressly been delegated to the executive by the supreme legislative authority of Parliament. But it was not until the fourteenth century was well advanced that the difference became marked. The Confirmatio Chartarum, which was forced on Edward I in 1297, was in no sense an assertion of the principle that taxation must be based on representation, but rather a negation of any power in the Crown arbitrarily to levy any extraordinary aids. Fleta, writing in Edward I's reign, and describing 'the King's Council in Parliament', stresses its judicial functions, and does not mention the Commons. The year 1322 saw the repeal of the Ordinances of those Lords Ordainers who had wrested the power from the weak hands of Edward II, that unworthy son of Edward I, that king who, in G. K. Chesterton's words, 'fawned on Gaveston and ran away from Bruce', but this enactment declared the assent of Parliament as a whole, not of the Commons in particular, to be essential to legislation.

But eventually the power of the Commons rose to its full stature, and the consummation, foreshadowed during this period, hastened during the Lancastrian, Yorkist, and Tudor periods, threatened during the early Stuart period, and finally reached at the Glorious Revolution of 1688, was the supremacy of the legislature over both the executive and the judiciary, in the sense that the recorded decision of the first-named organ, in the shape of an Act of Parliament, could at will increase, decrease, or destroy the activities of the two last-named. Thus we arrive at Austin's axiom, that there can be no legal limits to the power of a person, or body of persons, fulfilling the conditions requisite to justify the appellation of sovereign.

But between theory and practice there is a wide divergence. On the rock of strict law have accumulated the limpets of tradition and the barnacles of constitutional understandings. Though theoretically the very existence of executive and judiciary depend on the caprice of an omnipotent legislature, yet in practice on the one hand the executive exercises in the legislature the decisive voice, and on the other hand the idea that the legislature should, at the instance of the executive, curtail the independence of the judiciary is unthinkable.

It is time to show how it came about that the three organs of government remained to a large extent interlocked, how each organ, having broken free of the common parent, continued to exercise more than one part of that parent's functions.

(a) *The predominance of the executive in the legislature*

In the medieval period, the king in a real sense carried on the government of the country. The doctrine of ministerial counter-signature was yet unborn. This is not to say that the king could rule without ministers, or that ministers were not of great importance. A king might be a continual absentee, like Richard I, a minor for a period of years, like Henry III or Richard II, a lunatic like Henry VI at the end of his reign. That England was well governed through the reign of Richard I, and during the minority of Henry III, was due to the presence of two great ministers, Hubert Walter and Hubert de Burgh. The absence of any strong minister in the disastrous times of Henry VI invited chaos, and led to the senseless and ruinous Wars of the Roses.

Who were those ministers and what positions did they occupy? We must rid ourselves of the temptation to look at the Middle Ages through modern lenses, and antedate the modern Cabinet system, which is no older than the second half of the seventeenth century. The Prime Minister, who today overshadows all other high officers of State, would not be brought to life until 1714, as the result of the accession of a king who could speak no English. The highest minister of the early Middle Ages, the second man in the kingdom, was the justiciar. Glanvil, to whom is attributed the earliest treatise on English law, the forerunner of Bracton, was the justiciar of Henry II. The two great Huberts filled the same office, and bore the burden of State, the one on behalf of an absentee, the other on behalf of an infant king. But the history of the justiciarship, though glorious, was brief. It disappeared in the middle of the thirteenth century. The office which, though its beginning was less spectacular, was destined to play a far more important role, to be, indeed, the only office that has gone from one holder to another in unbroken succession from 1066 to the present day, embellished and dignified by the tenure of the Great Seal, is that of Chancellor.

The modern Lord Chancellor, in W. S. Gilbert's phrase, 'embodies the law'; he is at the pinnacle of the whole judicial hierarchy, and he presides over the sittings of the House of Lords. But in medieval times the Chancellor's activities ranged over the whole field of government. He has been described by Maitland, in a phrase which admits of no improvement, as the 'secretary of state for all departments'. As early as the beginning of Edward I's reign, he stands clearly at the head of the Chancery, the secretarial department of the Curia Regis. He, and he alone, could set free the remedial springs of the common law, for an intending litigant could not proceed without obtaining from the Chancery the appropriate royal writ. Thus he comes into prominence firstly as an executive officer. But his executive functions were later outstripped by the judicial functions which, emanating naturally from him as the 'keeper of the King's conscience', originated the system of equity, and turned the Chancery into the court which enunciated that system, side by side with the Common Pleas, King's Bench, and Exchequer, which enunciated the common law.

Parallel with the Chancery, the secretarial department, was the Exchequer, the financial department. At its head was the Treasurer, the second great officer of State. We shall see that his judicial, as well as executive, functions loomed large, for he was the head of the Court of Exchequer, but his office is now in commission, that is to say, it is held no longer by one man, but by several Lords of the Treasury, consisting of the First Lord, who is almost invariably the Prime Minister, the Chancellor of the Exchequer, in whose hands rests the chief burden of administration, and the Junior Lords, who act as Government Whips in the House of Commons. We are still reminded of the judicial functions of the Treasurer in the annual attendance in court by the Chancellor of the Exchequer for the purpose of the 'pricking of the sheriffs', that is to say, the designation of one out of three nominees to serve in the office for the ensuing year.

The composition of the body of colleagues who, with these two, made up the Council was, prior to the accession of Henry VI in 1422, indefinite and fluid, but during the long minority of that king it crystallized, and came to consist of the other four great officers of State, that is to say, the Keeper of the Great Seal, the Keeper of the Privy Seal, the Chamberlain, and the Steward of the Household, the Archbishops of Canterbury and York, and about fifteen other members. Secretaries of State do not emerge until the time of the Tudors, and we are still three centuries from the Prime Minister.

The Tudors have been called 'constitutional despots'. It might perhaps rather be said, with a mixture of cynicism and truth, that when they strayed from constitutional paths they were adroit enough to cover up their tracks. Henry VII, Henry VIII, and Elizabeth I all had a thorough understanding of the English people, and never persisted in any policy in face of their antagonism, as expressed in Parliament. They never allowed a difference to harden into a deadlock. At the same time they governed with the aid of a reformed and highly efficient Council, and such was the wisdom of their system of government that the spirit of conflict between executive and legislature slumbered until the Tudor dynasty had passed into history, and the throne of England was occupied by a Scottish king who understood her not at all.

During the reign of Henry VIII the executive and judicial functions of the Council tended to become separated and specialized. The former fell to an inner ring which grew up within the Council, and had long before his time been known as the Privy Council, the latter to the Council sitting at Westminster, that is to say, the Court of Star Chamber. The Privy Council gave birth, in turn, to a yet more intimate body of executive advisers, the

Cabinet, which was destined, as a result of the gradual elaboration of the system of party government during the eighteenth century, to provide the motive force of the House of Commons.

This book is a treatise on the judiciary, and our account of the other two organs of government must be limited to the minimum necessary for the portrayal of the courts in their correct setting. It must be sufficient here once more to emphasize the vital significance of the land law in English constitutional history. As long as the king, secure in the enjoyment of his feudal revenues, was financially dependent on Parliament only when abnormal expenditure demanded an extraordinary grant, so long were his ministers responsible only to him. Parliament could animadvert on their conduct only through the cumbersome and melodramatic process of impeachment, that is to say, trial by the House of Lords, on the accusation of the House of Commons. But when military tenures were abolished in 1660, Parliament gained virtually the entire control of that financial fuel without which the engine of State could not be kept in motion, and their exclusive sway over all matters relative to taxation was reasserted by the Bill of Rights in 1689. Had the famous clause of the Act of Settlement 1701, which excluded from the Commons all those holding places of profit under the Crown, ever taken actual effect, one of two results would have followed: either the king would, as Maitland suggests, have called all his ministers to the House of Lords, or else Britain would have forestalled the United States in the complete separation of Cabinet and Commons. But it never did take effect, for it was replaced, before it was due to come into force, by another provision of more limited and specialized import, which left the holders of many major offices fully eligible for a seat in the House. So, with the growth of the party system, and the hardening of party discipline, the Cabinet has gained a more and more dominant position in the House of Commons. A government with an absolute majority is in practice sure of the passage of any measure which it deems vital to its policy, and in recent years it has become apparent that a minority government can, by careful fostering of informal alliances with small parties in the Commons, achieve very nearly the same success. At the same time, the most docile House will keep a watchful eye on the conduct of the government as a whole, and on the administration by its members of their various departments, and can exercise, in the last resort, an infallible restraint through the refusal of supplies.

The most interesting aspect, from the judicial point of view, of the doctrine of collective ministerial responsibility to Parliament, rests in the nature of the sanction for maladministration. Though love of pageantry ranks high among English emotions, it is kept in check by an equally strong national sense of humour. Danby, for his negotiation of the Treaty of Dover in 1678, was impeached, and brought into danger of the block. But the public reprobation of the high-handed official treatment of the son-in-law of the former owner of land at Crichel Down, which had been requisitioned before the Second World War, and which was no longer needed by the Crown, was vindicated in 1954 by the resignation of the Minister of Agriculture. In America, as ministers do not sit in Congress, and cannot therefore be publicly questioned by it, impeachment is a weapon kept continually sharpened for contemporary needs. The process of impeachment of a President or any other civil officer is expressly provided for in Article II of the United States Constitution, and its threatened use brought about the resignation of President Nixon in 1974.

In Britain impeachment in practice is completely obsolete. The last impeachment was that of Lord Melville in 1808, and it is unthinkable that the process should ever be used again. In any case the office of Parliamentary Commissioner was created by an Act of 1967. His task is to inquire into individual allegations of maladministration by government departments, and to suggest methods of righting any wrongs which he may find to have been perpetrated. This office is modelled on that of the Danish Ombudsman, which has been the pattern for many similar offices in various other countries. Indeed, even in the United Kingdom, other 'ombudsmen' have been set up since 1967, including a National Health Service Commissioner[3] and Commissions for Local Administration,[4] the latter investigating alleged maladministration in local government. The extra-judicial remedies afforded by these sundry officers are an important feature of the modern state.

---

[3] Created by the National Health Service Reorganization Act 1973.
[4] Created by the Local Government Act 1974.

(b) *The dual function of the House of Lords, as the upper house of the legislature, and the highest law court*

We have had occasion more than once to emphasize that the English Constitution has never reached a complete specialization of the legislative, executive, and judicial functions. There has always been a certain amount of overlap. For the discharge of executive functions Parliament, as the result of an unsuccessful attempt to govern through committees during the Civil War, recognized its own unfitness. But it was in the Middle Ages, as Professor McIlwain emphasizes, primarily a court of law, the High Court of Parliament. So it arrogated to itself and retained certain judicial functions of the highest importance. The settlement of these judicial functions forms an important chapter in its history. Coke uttered a misleading half-truth when he said: 'The Lords in their House have power of judicature, and the Commons in their House have power of judicature, and both Houses together have power of judicature.' For the attitude of the Commons, in denying to the Lords original civil jurisdiction in 1666, in the case of *Skinner* v. *East India Company*, was purely negative; they were claiming such jurisdiction, not for themselves, but for the common law courts. For themselves they have never claimed higher powers than are bounded by their jurisdiction to commit persons for contempt, and to determine the constitution of their own body. They also have the quasi-judicial initiative in impeachment. Acting together, the Houses can present to the king an address for the removal of a judge or the Comptroller and Auditor-General, or a Bill of Attainder, stating *ex post facto* that a person has committed a crime. When we speak of the High Court of Parliament we mean, in practice, the House of Lords.

Since 1666 the House of Lords has claimed no original civil jurisdiction except in cases of privilege, which are of no great importance. The Committee of Privileges of the House can decide on the effect or validity of the creation of a new peerage by the Crown or on other matters affecting the constitution of the House. Thus the Sex Disqualification Removal Act 1919 left it uncertain whether a peeress in her own right was thereby entitled to sit in the House of Lords. In 1922 Viscountess Rhondda, on behalf of the women in that position, who then numbered twenty-nine, raised the question before the Committee of Privileges, who decided it in the negative. But her efforts eventually reaped a reward, for the Life Peerages Act 1958 empowers the Crown to create 'any person' a baron for life, with a seat in the House, while the Peerage Act 1963 grants to all hereditary peeresses of the realm[5] the right to membership of the House. The Lords can also decide on a disputed claim to an old peerage, but only if the case has been referred to it by the Crown.

With the abolition, by the Criminal Justice Act 1948, of the trial of a peer by his peers for treason or felony, the original criminal jurisdiction of the House is limited to impeachment, which may to all intents and purposes be called obsolete.

Of far greater importance is the appellate jurisdiction. The House is the final court of appeal in civil matters from all courts of appeal in England, Scotland, Wales, and Northern Ireland. At the risk of anticipating our discussion of the dual system of common law and equity, it must be said that in the seventeenth century the Commons resisted the claim of the Lords to hear appeals from the equity side of the Court of Chancery. It was not until 1675 that, as the outcome of the case of *Shirley* v. *Fagg*, the House finally vindicated the exercise of this jurisdiction. But to the appellate, as opposed to the original, common law jurisdiction of the House no objection was ever raised. Only the *method* of appeal has undergone a beneficial change. Between the time of Edward IV and 1875 it was by the complicated and unsatisfactory procedure of writ of error, but in that year this procedure was abandoned under the Judicature Act 1873, which replaced it by the adoption of the more rational method of a rehearing of the case, which the Chancery had always employed.

The Criminal Appeal Act 1907 renders the House a final court of appeal in criminal matters[6] from the Court of Criminal Appeal (or, since the Criminal Appeal Act 1966, the new criminal division of the Court of Appeal), and by the Administration of Justice Act 1960 a case can be taken, at the instance of either the defendant or the prosecutor, to the House wherever the lower appellate court certifies that a point of law of general public importance is

---

[5] Irish peers and peeresses are, however, excluded from membership.

[6] The Lords may now entertain criminal appeals from England, Wales, and Northern Ireland, but not from Scotland.

involved, and it appears either to that court or to the House of
Lords that the point is one which ought to be considered by the
House. Thus in *R.* v. *Woolmington* in 1935, the defence of the
prisoner to a charge of murder was that the gun went off by
accident. The trial judge directed the jury, following the authority
of a case of the middle of the nineteenth century, that once the
Crown had discharged its duty of establishing that the deceased
met her death at the hands of the prisoner, the burden of proof
shifted, and it became the duty of the prisoner to show that the
circumstances causing the death fell short of constituting murder.
The prisoner having been convicted, and the conviction upheld by
the Court of Criminal Appeal, the House upset it, thus finally
overruling the authority relied on by the trial judge. The effect of
the decision is that the presumption of the prisoner's innocence
prevails throughout the entire course of a trial for homicide; the
jury must weigh against one another the alternative explanations
of the death advanced by the Crown and the prisoner. But another
presumption, which in its own field is equally strong, concerns the
defence of diminished responsibility under the Homicide Act 1957;
if the prisoner pleads the defence, it is incumbent on him to
establish it; and the same may be said, on the authority of *Reg.* v.
Podola in 1959, of amnesia.

The House of Lords, whatever its business, is still the same
House, and its sessions as a final appellate court preserve in theory
the character of a debate. Thus one speaks of the opinions delivered as *speeches*, and not as *judgments*, though since 1963 the
practice of reading them aloud *in extenso* in the House has largely
been abandoned. Now it is normal for the bare decision to be
pronounced orally, and the detailed speeches are then available in
printed form. According to strict law, any Lord of Parliament can
sit, and in earlier times lay Lords actually did so, but usage has
now established a rule, which will certainly never be broken, that
nobody without defined legal qualifications ever sits. Thus in
practice the judges are the Lord Chancellor, any ex-Lord Chancellors, any Lord who is holding or has held high judicial office, and,
most important of all, the Lords of Appeal in Ordinary. These last
are appointed by the Crown under the powers conferred on it by
the Appellate Jurisdiction Acts 1876 and 1947. They are life peers,
until 1958 the only ones in the House. In that year Parliament at

last gave effect to a proposal which was, as Bagehot reminds us, made at the time of the Reform Act 1832, but which foundered on the rock of opposition led by Lord Lyndhurst.

When we speak of the judicial opinions of members of the House of Lords as speeches, we preserve the legacy of history. But the demands of common sense and of humanity may legitimately prevail over those of theoretical symmetry, particularly in criminal cases. This was one of the lessons taught us by *Joyce* v. *Director of Public Prosecutions* in 1946. Joyce was accused of treason in respect of his notorious broadcast talks from Germany during the 1939–45 war. A very difficult point of law was raised by the undoubted fact that, at the time of the alleged offences, he was neither a British subject nor resident within British jurisdiction. He was nevertheless convicted on the ground of his continued possession of a valid British passport, though it had expired by the time of his arrest. On this point an appeal was taken to the Court of Criminal Appeal, where the conviction was affirmed. On the final appeal to the House of Lords, the House decided, by a majority, that the appeal ought to be dismissed. Clearly the preparation of their speeches, on an issue of such importance, must take some time. Must Joyce be kept in suspense? Humanity forbade, and the speeches were delivered after his execution. Again, in the case of *Harris* in 1952, the speeches were postponed until after the House had intimated that his appeal against conviction for larceny[7] would be allowed. The present practice of not reading the speeches out would seem to be likely to make this procedure uniform in criminal cases.

The personalities of the judges of the Supreme Court of the United States are far better known to the American public than are those of the judicial members of the House of Lords to the British public. The reason is that, as the powers of Congress are defined by the Constitution, to the Supreme Court falls the vital function of deciding whether a piece of legislation is in or out of harmony with the Constitution. Therefore, the life of an Act of Congress must always be, in a sense, precarious until the Supreme Court has pronounced on its robustness, though such pronouncement will never be made if no one is sufficiently aggrieved by it to bring an

---

[7] The crime of larceny was abolished by the Theft Act 1968, and replaced by that of theft.

issue before the Court involving its validity. This function of the Supreme Court necessarily renders it, especially at times when legislation of a controversial character has been passed by Congress, the cynosure of all eyes. It is the absence of this function which renders the judicial work of the House of Lords much less spectacular. Yet, in the narrower field of interpretation, the work of the House is most important. On the development of private law, too, its work has an enormous impact, much more so than is the case with its American counterpart, for in America the field of private law mostly belongs to the State Courts. Another difference which has existed between the two Courts is that, while the Supreme Court can reverse its own decisions, it was established in 1898 that the House of Lords could not do so. This latter rule was relaxed by the Lords themselves in 1966, and the House may now depart from its previous decisions if there is good reason to do so. It is indispensable that the Lords of Appeal in Ordinary should be drawn from the ablest lawyers of the day, as a majority decision of the House can upset a unanimous judgment of the Court of Appeal affirming that of a trial judge. The calibre of three judges whose decision can prevail over that of six must needs be great.

(c) *The blend of judicial and executive functions in the Judicial Committee of the Privy Council*

When the Long Parliament in 1641 abolished the Court of Star Chamber it was but exercising its undoubted and absolute legislative power. But where it would have been completely justified in giving no reason at all for its action, it chose to make itself ridiculous by giving a reason at variance with the facts of history. For the preamble to the Statute alleged that the Court had been created by the Act *pro Camera Stellata* of 1487, and had over-stepped the powers entrusted to it by that Act. But it was far older than the Act of 1487. Its existence was recognized and commended by that stalwart champion of the common law, Coke, in his *Fourth Institute*, the greatest of all commentaries on the courts. For it was simply the name given to the court which exercised the judicial powers of the Council, whose history might be summarized as follows. In the medieval period it was a somewhat vague and heterogeneous body, which from the reign of Edward III onwards tended to become more definite. It had a very wide, albeit undefined, jurisdiction, but it aroused the jealousy and suspicion of the common lawyers and of Parliament by reason of its identification with the Crown and the prerogative, and of the fact that its procedure was very different from that of the common law. In deference to the Commons, it ceased in 1351 to examine defendants on oath. Between that date and 1453, petitions were brought and statutes enacted against the Council, but their effect was rather to recognize than to limit its jurisdiction. By 1453, when the last and crowning statute was passed, the Council had grown strong, but its powerful members took advantage of the imbecility of Henry VI to forward their own interests. Personal ambition usurped the place that should have been occupied by national policy, and government by the Council proved anything but a success. The period of the Wars of the Roses was a period of anarchy, during which neither the Council nor any other body exercised any continuity of control. It revived during the reign of Edward IV, but Richard III, in exclaiming that 'Now is the winter of our discontent made glorious summer by this sun of York', was exhibiting a somewhat premature optimism. For the Council had lost its cohesion, and had reverted, in its composition, to the elusive and kaleidoscopic character of an earlier age. The accession of Henry VII marks the final triumph of order over the chaos of factional strife that had torn the country for too long a span of time. The majority of the Council had been Yorkist not only in allegiance but also in sympathy, and had blithely acquiesced in setting a price on his head. Though he had hit upon the Council as his medium of government, the Council he envisaged was one that had undergone the process which, in the jargon of modern political phraseology, is known as a purge. The Act *pro Camera Stellata* of 1487 represents the first step taken by him towards the furtherance of his object. It was essentially an empirical measure. What it established was not, of course, the Court of Star Chamber, which, though temporarily in abeyance, retained all the judicial powers of the Council apart from those taken from it by the series of statutes ranging over the century 1351–1453, but a strong committee of the Council to deal with offences imperilling the safety of the State. This committee was endowed with the power, which the Star Chamber had relinquished in 1351, of examining the defendant and witnesses on oath. There is no record that this committee ever actually sat, and

by Henry VIII's reign it had become redundant, for the process of
purgation had now run its full cycle, and the Court of Star
Chamber was ready and equipped to perform all the work envisaged for the committee established by the Act of 1487. During the
remainder of the Tudor period it grew from strength to strength, as
a most efficient and popular court. It dealt mainly with matters
concerning the safety of the State, but also with many other
matters, some falling within, others outside the common law, such
as foreign trade, defamation, fraud, and forgery. The procedure
was not as in the common law courts, by writ, but by bill, as in the
Court of Chancery. The vital difference between the writ and the
bill was that whereas the former specified the entire scope of
complaint against the defendant, the latter summoned him to
answer not only as to matters specified therein, but as to other
unspecified matters as well. The Star Chamber further resembled the
Chancery, and differed from the courts of common law, in that
juries were unknown in it. Its bounds are commonly said to have
been marked by cases of freehold and felony; it did not claim to
decide the title to freehold land, and it tried and punished only
misdemeanours. As it did not deal with felonies, it follows that it
never passed the death sentence.[8]

The Act of 1641, which abolished the Court of Star Chamber,
left to the Council its appellate jurisdiction from the overseas
possession of the Crown. These were at that time very few, consisting of Virginia, Newfoundland, the Channel Islands, and only a
few other places. Cromwell was, in Professor G. M. Trevelyan's
words, the first Englishman to think imperially. From this time
onwards the Empire increased in extent, and more and more red
colouring appeared on the map of the world, thus swelling the
volume of the work of the Appeal Committee of the Council. In
1833 was passed an Act 'for the better administration of justice in
His Majesty's Privy Council', establishing the modern Judicial
Committee, which is the final court of appeal from the Ecclesiastical Courts, the Prize Court, the General Medical and General
Dental Councils, and those parts of the Commonwealth the decisions of whose highest Courts are not final. It also may be called

[8] The death penalty for murder was abolished by the Murden (Abolition of
Death Penalty) Act 1965, and the classification of crimes as felonies and misdemeanours by the Criminal Law Act 1967.

upon by the Secretary of State for Scotland, under the Scotland Act 1978, to decide whether any Bill passed by the Scottish Assembly is within its area of legislative competence, though it is now doubtful whether this Act will ever be brought into force.

The Judicial Committee is not only a court of law properly so called; it also exercises the executive power of the Crown to hear petitions. A subject appealing to it is, notionally, applying to the King to redress a grievance which has found no alleviation in the ordinary courts of his country. The King naturally refers such an application to the body of legal advisers provided for him by the Act of 1833. It would perhaps be odd for those advisers to speak with discordant voices, and that is the reason why the Judicial Committee, although its composition is for practical purposes almost identical with that of the members of the House of Lords who hear appeals, has in the past enunciated only one opinion, whereas it is by no means uncommon to find the House of Lords divided by three to two, or even four to three. Yet in 1966 it was announced that in future dissenting opinions would, where appropriate, be given, which perhaps illustrates the pragmatic way in which our institutions sometimes develop.

5 The courts of common law and their several functions – 1

It has taken four chapters to divest the judicial body of its legislative and executive garments, and the divesting process has been only partial, for some of the garments have been sewn on to the body by the logic of history, and form an integral part of it. The persistent state of mutual interdependence among the three organs of governments renders very difficult a systematic arrangement of the subject-matter of an account of the judicial system. Thus, though we have already said something about the shire court and sheriff's tourn, which operated below the level of the three common law courts, of the House of Lords, which rose above them, and of the Court of Star Chamber, which until 1641 played the part of their serious rival, whose struggle with them was literally a struggle to the death, we have said little of those three courts themselves. These are, so to speak, the infantry of the judicial line, through whose rifles we are now free to fire at point-blank range.

We have remarked that the Norman kings found the sheriff the ruler of the shire; the very eminence of his position rendered him a useful instrument for their purposes. While preserving, and even increasing, his dignity, they converted him, in effect, from a president into a viceroy. Maitland's brilliant statement that 'The whole history of English justice and police might be brought under this rubric, "The Decline and Fall of the Sheriff"' emphasizes that the tendency of the process of events was to erase his former, and paint in vivid colours his latter character. The following reflections may serve as strokes of the brush, which will present a not inaccurate picture of the change in his position.

(a) Any appearance of autonomy in the counties was rendered delusive by the growth of a system of rigid central supervision. From a position of irresponsibility in local administration, the sheriff passed under the discipline of a periodical scrutiny by omniscient royal officials. Members of a modern local authority, being surcharged for unlawful expenditure by district auditors sent from the Department of the Environment, are but playing their parts in an age-old drama, whereof the theme of the first act was the inquisition and censure of the actions of the sheriff by the justices of the General Eyre. These justices tried a few local criminals, but the bulk of their work consisted in overhauling every detail of local administration since the last eyre, and inflicting heavy fines for trifling incidents of maladministration. General Eyres ceased during the first half of the fourteenth century, but they had most successfully fulfilled their purpose, of the complete subordination of the local to the central authority; and the necessity for rigid supervision, once learned, was never forgotten, though it came to be exercised by other and less cumbersome means.

(*b*) The sheriff retained, until the reign of Mary I, his control over the Armed Forces of the shire. But that queen instituted lords-lieutenant, who took over those powers, only to yield them, in 1907, to the newly created Territorial Associations, which Parliament had brought into being at the instance of Lord Haldane.

(*c*) He retained for a longer period his 'police powers' of arrest and committal. But these were eventually taken over from him by the system of regular police forces evolved in the nineteenth century by the work of Peel.

(*d*) But the sheriff is chiefly interesting in his courts. Their fortunes inevitably waxed and waned with those of the sheriff himself. The shire court has had a most curious history. In the early Norman period it partook, at the times of the visits of the king's itinerant justices, of the character of a Curia Regis in miniature, vigorous in all three functions of government; but later it fell, not so much into disfavour as into oblivion, and was left imperceptibly to fade out of life through inanition. As a result of the assertion by Henry II of the principle that serious crime belonged to the Curia Regis alone, it had been shorn of all its criminal jurisdiction as early as the beginning of the thirteenth century. Its civil jurisdiction received a staggering blow through the interpretation put upon the Statute of Gloucester 1278, that it should have no jurisdiction if the amount at stake exceeded forty shillings, and was beaten to the ground by the flanking attacks of the writ of *pone*. Criminal jurisdiction, in the case of trivial crime, remained for some time to the sheriff's other court, the sheriff's tourn, but the rise of the justices of the peace tended gradually to appropriate the whole of it, and this tendency was recognized by an Act of 1461, which provided that indictments for crimes justiciable by it were thenceforth to be brought before the justices of the peace. Yet an Act of the Parliament of Richard III in 1484 regulated the quality of its jurors, and the tourn was not officially abolished until 1887.

As regards legislative powers, it is almost superfluous to reiterate that the English constitution has never shown any sort of tendency to develop along federal lines. The effect of the growth of a sovereign Parliament was to kill all local legislatures, though a subordinate Parliament for the province of Northern Ireland was specially created and lasted for some fifty years in the present century, and the recently enacted Scotland Act 1978 and Wales Act 1978 made provision for subordinate Assemblies to be set up in those two provinces if local referendums proved that there was sufficient popular support for such innovations. Any rules and orders made by modern county councils, which date from 1888, are made under powers conferred upon them by Parliament, and a judge may be called upon to test their validity by the touchstone of the doctrine of *ultra vires*.

From the time of Edward I onwards, the common law was evolved by the decisions of the courts of Common Pleas, King's Bench, and Exchequer, and of the itinerant justices. We must look at the work of each of these agencies. There was never any nice allocation of jurisdiction between them. Rather do we find that the officials of each were continually astute to make inroads, overt and covert, on the territories of the others, impelled by the remorseless logic of a system of judicial piecework. The more cases a court tried, the more fees accrued to its officials, and so none of the three courts could rest content with the jurisdiction that fell legitimately to its share. The spoliations of King's Bench and Exchequer had almost pushed Common Pleas off the edge of existence, when it was saved in the seventeenth century by the bold counter-attacks of Chief Justice North, whose result was to render the jurisdiction of the three courts virtually co-ordinate.

We have seen that Magna Carta laid down that Common Pleas should sit always at a fixed place. This static quality differentiated it sharply from King's Bench, which, as the name implies, followed the King on his progresses as long as such progresses continued to be made. To Common Pleas fell naturally the writ of right, and the personal actions of debt and detinue. It had nothing to do with crime. It is necessary here to say something about the process of trial. No unfaithful summary of it is provided by the four words of the Queen of Hearts, 'Sentence first; verdict afterwards.' In the wonderland of the early Middle Ages a trial partook largely of the nature of an appeal to the supernatural. The plaintiff must first produce his *secta*, a body of friends who testified orally to the genuineness of his case. The defendant having also made an oral defence, the court would give a *medial judgment*, that is to say it would officially record that the issue had been defined, and the facts of the case must go for trial by a method of proof which it would prescribe. The method prescribed for the writ of right was trial by battle, which was also, as we have seen, the proper method for a criminal appeal of felony. The old personal actions were tried by compurgation, or wager of law. This institution rested on a traditional view of public regard for the sanctity of oaths which was belied by the lightness of contemporary practice. A defendant who was sufficiently hardened to swear a false oath, and obtained the support of the false oaths of twelve 'compurgators', would inevitably defeat the plaintiff's case. The plaintiff could win only by attacking, not the veracity of the compurgators, but their adherence to correct ritual. An oath sworn in correct form was final; if the wrong words were sworn, it was valueless. Thus battle laid a premium on brute strength, compurgation on bold perjury.

The dubiety of the methods by which these actions were tried naturally detracted from their popularity, and provided for the King's Bench the first suggestion of the vulnerability of the Common Pleas. The work of King's Bench was, from the first, concerned with the pleas of the Crown, which, thanks to the work of Henry II, tended more and more to be tried by jury. The only contact of King's Bench with trial by battle was in criminal cases in which recourse was had to the old procedure by appeal, which, though not abolished until 1819, steadily lost ground to the robust procedure by indictment, which necessarily involved trial by jury. But the genius of legal history ruled that the bulk of the work of the King's Bench should be, in practice, not criminal but civil. For the adminstration of criminal justice became early decentralized, serious crime falling to the itinerant justices of oyer and terminer and General Gaol Delivery, familiarly known as 'the assizes', and trivial crime being disposed of, at first by the sheriff's tourn, and later by the justices of the peace, who eventually absorbed the entire work of that court. It was only in comparatively infrequent cases that crime was actually tried by King's Bench itself. But it was precisely the criminal jurisdiction of the court that gave it civil jurisdiction. For the action of trespass, the corner-stone of that jurisdiction, was an offspring of the criminal law. Through the action of case, it was capable of, and achieved, a vast expansion in the field, not only of contract and tort, but of the land law as well. We must remember two things: firstly that it started with the large initial advantage that, while the other actions, triable in the Common Pleas, were harnessed to the bad old forms of trial, trespass at no time knew any form but trial by jury, and secondly that it was a weapon, to which until the middle of the seventeenth century Common Pleas found no foil, admirably suited to enable the King's Bench to prise open the treasure-house of its rival and, by appropriating its jurisdiction, denude it of its fees.

King's Bench increased its civil jurisdiction at the expense of Common Pleas, partly by the legitimate method of expanding trespass and *case* into newer actions which would do more efficiently the work of the older actions, and partly by the more questionable use of legal fictions in order to capture even those actions themselves.

We have mentioned Covenant, the action for the breach of a contract under seal. We are today so familiar with the idea that contract pervades our lives, that every agreement, to which the parties must be taken to have intended that binding legal force shall attach, is enforceable by a court of law, that it comes as a shock to us to recall that in the early medieval period things were very different. In order that an agreement should attain the dignity of an enforceable contract, it was necessary that it should be attended with the formality of a seal, which was the English equivalent of the set form of words prescribed by the Roman Law for the contract of *stipulatio*.[1] In the calendar of medieval litigation, at least so far as the royal courts were concerned, the simple,

---

[1] 'Spondesne?' 'Spondeo.' ('Do you promise?' 'I do promise.')

informal contract of modern life found no place. But when the action of *case*, the branch of trespass, grew to maturity, it then in turn put out shoots.

The most vivid contemporary account of the medieval common law is the series of reports known as the Year Books, which range from the reign of Edward I to that of Henry VIII. The view generally accepted today is that they were in no sense official, but compiled by lawyers and students attending the courts. Through the welter of cases, and the commentaries thereon by legal and historical scholars, runs the scarlet thread by which the simple contract won its way to the light, and thus enabled the commercial law to keep pace with social needs. That thread was the great action of *assumpsit*. If Jones agreed to ferry Smith's horse over a river, and in the course of the journey the horse fell into the water through the negligence of the ferryman, what would be the appropriate form of action? Clearly *case*, as it was not suggested that the horse had been pushed in, and a situation falling short of this was outside the sphere of trespass. But what if the horse had, in spite of Jones's promise, never started on its journey, but had been left on the bank? Unless the agreement had been under seal, Smith was left without a remedy. But the growth of commercial enterprise, which cannot rest on the collapsible foundations of moral obligation, brought lawyers to the realization of the vital necessity for a sure remedy for the breach of an ordinary business undertaking. Such a breach might take the form either of a misfeasance, a failure in the course of performance, or of a non-feasance, an entire failure to embark on performance. Misfeasance came to be viewed from two alternative aspects, that of indirect damage to property, and that of breach of contract. According as the former or the latter aspect were stressed, case or assumpsit would be the appropriate action. But non-feasance fell right outside the purview of case, and belonged to assumpsit alone. It had become established by the middle of the sixteenth century that assumpsit could always be brought for the breach of a simple contract, provided only that it were fortified by *consideration*, which was evolved as an acid test of its validity. This vital ingredient consists of a detriment to the promisee, that is to say, a sensible change of position by him in reliance on the promise. Sir William Holdsworth has shown that, while benefit to the promisor is not indispensable to a simple contract, without detriment to the promisee it cannot live. The detriment may be merely nominal, but it must be real, and enjoy present vitality. It may be constituted by the delivery by the promisee of a document devoid of value, or by the performance of a contract already entered into by him with a third party. But a past consideration is no consideration; that is to say, no action can be brought for a reward promised in return for services already rendered, for here the detriment had spent itself and expired before the date of the contract.

The evolution of assumpsit enormously increased the jurisdiction of King's Bench, but not yet at the expense of Common Pleas, except in so far as it tended to reduce the numbers of contracts under seal. To these, of course, the doctrine of consideration has never had any application, simply because the action of covenant was well established long before it even entered the realm of juristic thought. The trite and fatuous statement that consideration is not required in a contract under seal because 'the seal imports consideration' is just as unhistorical as it would be to say that a Roman scythe-bearing chariot did not require a carburettor because the presence of the scythe imported a carburettor!

Flushed with its success, assumpsit sought a new field of conquest, and soon found it in the action of debt, which, after some decades of hot strife, it succeeded in overwhelming through the entire occupation of its territory. Debts often arise from agreement; why not, therefore, gain further jurisdiction for assumpsit by simply stressing, not the debt itself, but the promise to pay it? So far victory was bloodless; but what if there were no promise to pay the debt? King's Bench insisted that a promise must be implied. Clearly for Common Pleas to concede this point would be tantamount to judicial suicide, which Common Pleas was in no mood to commit. Nevertheless in *Slade's Case* in 1602 the decisive battle was fought, and won by King's Bench. Thenceforth debt, though it continued to make fitful appearances until the early part of the nineteenth century, had been drained of all its elixir of life. Compurgation, its inseparable incubus, was fatal to its popularity, and all but a few sentimental antiquarians turned from it with joy to a new action wherein trial by jury flourished.

But the appetite of King's Bench was insatiable. Not content with by-passing the action of debt, it also continued the process, which had been begun some time before *Slade's Case*, of working for its capture by frontal attack. Its weapon here was the legal fiction, which Maine, as we have seen, described as the first of the three agencies whereby the law is brought into harmony with the needs of society. Legal fictions are of two kinds, historic and dogmatic. With the latter we are not here concerned, though they are of prime importance in general jurisprudence; they are the means whereby legal phenomena are brought under a collective formula, and of them the so-called 'fiction-theory' of corporate personality, the child of the brain of Pope Innocent IV, provides a good example.[2] But the device of an historic fiction enables a desire for change to be gratified without offence to some scruple of legal conservatism which makes men unwilling to give to their desire articulate expression. Often it has been the first step towards, and the harbinger of, legislation. It is even true to say that the device is sometimes implicit in legislation itself. It is so in the Summer Time Act. Compulsory regulation of our hour of rising would be a tyranny from which the most absolute of dictators might shrink. But by simply calling six o'clock seven o'clock the object is achieved with ease, if not without some criticism.

King's Bench wished to draw debt into its net. It therefore issued to the Sheriff of Middlesex a writ, known as the Bill of Middlesex, alleging that the defendant had committed a trespass, and was to be arrested and brought before the court if found in Middlesex. If the sheriff replied that the defendant *non est inventus*, that is to say, is not in Middlesex, King's Bench persevered, and issued to the sheriff of Berkshire a variant of the Bill of Middlesex called the writ of *latitat*, which recited that the defendant was concealed in Berkshire, and so he would be hunted from county to county until he was ultimately run to earth. Once he had been brought before the court, it would then proceed to try the action of debt. A Statute of 1661 spiked the court's guns by providing that no arrest could take place unless the writ set forth the true cause of action. The setback was but temporary, for King's Bench found it childishly easy to circumvent the Statute, by the *ac etiam* process, that is to say, the addition to the statement of the cause of action in the writ of a clause alleging that the defendant had *also* committed

---

[2] See Gray, *Nature and Sources of the Law*, p. 35.

a trespass. This process of course must have lost much of its practical utility after *Slade's Case*, though it was still employed. But we shall see that the weapon which King's Bench may have allowed to become rusty was taken up and polished by Common Pleas, which, under the inspiring leadership of Chief Justice North, entered in the second half of the seventeenth century into a fight for its very life.

But the ambitions of the King's Bench transcended the field of contract. On two other fronts it made important advances. We have seen that there has never been in English law a real action for the specific recovery of goods; for the detention of a chattel the appropriate action was detinue, whereby damages up to its value would be ordered in default of its restitution. It belonged, like debt, to Common Pleas. It was of two varieties, *detinue sur bailment and detinue sur trover*. The former lay in cases where the chattel had got into the defendant's hands through a bailment, under which important and comprehensive rubric are included all those various legal relationships which have the common feature that one person, the bailor, has entrusted a chattel to another person, the bailee, on the terms that the latter should do something with it and return it to the bailor. I lend my friend a book; I take my trousers to be pressed; I give my bulldog into the care of a veterinary surgeon during my absence abroad; I pawn my watch: all these transactions constitute bailments, involving a whole budget of varying rights and duties on the part of bailee and bailor. A refusal or failure by the bailee to return the chattel at the due time would involve him in the action of detinue. But detinue suffered from a grave defect, quite apart from the blemish of compurgation, which it shared with debt. It could be brought only for detention; it would not lie[3] for misuse of the chattel by the bailee, or its return by him in a damaged condition. These defects were common to *detinue sur trover* also, which lay where a chattel had got into the defendant's hands without any bailment. So in the sixteenth century *case*, which was already revolutionizing contract by the production of assumpsit, proceeded to give full scope for the development of the tort of conversion by putting out yet another offshoot, the action of *trover*. The form of this action was modelled on the procedure *per*

[3] This is the technical way of saying that an action could not be brought.

inventionem, involving a fictitious allegation of loss of the chattel by the plaintiff, and finding by the defendant, with which lawyers had been familiarized by *detinue sur trover*, with the addition of a further allegation that the defendant had converted it to his own use. Trover was free from the two defects that so hampered the utility of its original, and superseded detinue as assumpsit had superseded debt. And yet the analogy is not quite exact, for whereas debt wandered on the fringe of the law as an uneasy ghost, detinue remained a creature of flesh and blood, for it would lie in one case where trover would not, namely where the defendant, having once had possession of the chattel, had not converted it, but merely lost it through negligence. Thus it enjoyed continued vitality, especially after it had been purged of its worst blemish by the abolition of compurgation in 1833. Indeed, in 1854 it received from Parliament an access of dignity which had been until that date consistently denied to all personal actions, for the Common Law Procedure Act of that year empowered a judge to decree specific restitution. But though detinue proved of tougher fibre than debt, it undoubtedly played a far less important part in the law of torts than trover. At one time it seemed as if trover would take over the entire functions of trespass to goods, but its expansion in this direction was prevented by Chief Justice Pratt, who in the case of *Bushel* v. *Miller* in 1718 laid down that in order that trover should lie, it must be shown that the defendant had committed a conversion, that is to say arrogated to himself the functions of an owner; for a mere asportation[4] trespass only would lie. The practical difference was that a plaintiff could recover by trover the full value of the chattel, but by trespass only the actual damage suffered. It was not until 1977, by the Torts (Interference with Goods) Act, that detinue and other related causes of action were abolished and replaced by a single tort of wrongful interference with goods.

The curious result of the absence of a real action for chattels is that much of the law of personal property overlaps the law of torts; a personal action is brought to vindicate a real right. But the writ of right was also attacked by the irrepressible action of trespass, through its offspring ejectment. In order to understand this action,

---

[4] The technical word denoting the act of carrying away. It is one of the essential ingredients in the old crime of larceny, which by the Theft Act 1968 was replaced by the modern crime of theft.

it is necessary to return to the land law, and say something of leasehold. This was not a tenure, but the outcome of a contract. It had nothing to do with feudalism. Smith would simply agree under seal to let Jones occupy his land for a term of years in return for the payment of an annual rental. Jones acquired no real right in the land, but only a personal right against Smith. If ejected by Smith or any agent of his he could bring against him the action of covenant for the recovery of damages. Then about 1237 he was given a new writ, *quare ejecit infra terminum*, whereby he could recover the land itself. But against a stranger he had no protection until the action of trespass came into general use. By a form of trespass known as *ejectio firmae*, certainly from Edward II's reign onwards, he could recover damages from any stranger who had ejected him. But it was not until the very end of the fifteenth century that it was finally decided that by *ejectio firmae* the land itself, as well as damages, might be recovered. Thus leasehold attained an amphibious quality in that, though specifically recoverable, it continued to be classified as personal property, and descended as such on the intestacy of the tenant. This new action of *ejectment* became much coveted by the freeholder, for, like all offshoots of trespass, it was tried by jury. But in order to make it available to the freeholder it was necessary to have recourse to a fiction. Suppose B to be in possession of Blackacre, to which A claimed to be entitled. Now we have seen that the idea of seisin, which originally almost coincided with that of possession, gradually pushed further into the orbit of ownership. In the early Middle Ages, a disseisee very soon lost his right of entry, and was thrown back on the assize of novel disseisin, or the writ of right. But by the latter half of the fifteenth century, when Littleton wrote his monumental work on Tenures, to which Coke by his commentary ensured immortality, the dispossessed owner had attained a far more favourable postion. For it was only in rare cases that he lost his right of entry. A then did enter. Here fact ended and fiction began. On his entry he made a fictitious lease to a fictitious person, John Doe. Doe fictitiously entered and stayed on the land until fictitiously ousted by B. An action would then be brought against B, really of course by A, but ostensibly in the name of Doe. In this action A appeared only as the 'lessor of the plaintiff', Doe, who made four allegations, which, like those of loss and finding in the action of trover, B was not allowed to deny: (1) A's right to enter, (2) the lease by A to Doe, (3) Doe's entry under the lease, (4) Doe's ouster by B. In this way B's pleadings were confined to the merits of the case, and the question of title was tried out.

Thus in land, as in chattels, a personal action became available for the vindication of a real right, and a portion of the law of real property protruded itself into the territory of torts, which had already, as we have seen, undergone an occupation on a large scale by the law of personal property. The writ of right, for most purposes, was superseded by ejectment, and would be brought only where the latter had been barred, under the Limitation Act 1623, by the passage of twenty years; for the writ of right still fell under an Act of 1540, which barred it only after sixty years. Clause 34 of Magna Carta lost all its remaining significance in 1833, when the real actions were abolished by the Real Property Limitation Act.

A moment's reflection will serve to show the position of Common Pleas in the middle of the seventeenth century as almost desperate. Not one of the actions falling within its jurisdiction but had been reduced to a state of comparative impotence by the acquisitive tactics of King's Bench. Looking back on the situation from the vantage-ground of the twentieth century, one is inclined to regret that Common Pleas could not accept it, and realize that one court with comprehensive functions is better than two with different functions; that the activities of the King's Bench, though prompted only by the immediate desire to augment the fees of its officials, had nevertheless produced a result beneficial for the English judicial system in general. But no court would willingly acquiesce in its own annihilation, and the time was not yet ripe for amalgamation. Chief Justice North was quite determined not only to preserve Common Pleas but even to inspire it with new vigour. He conceived the bold plan of carrying the war into the enemy's country and fighting him with his own weapons. By the use of the Bill of Middlesex he captured the enemy's capital; for the procedure enabled Common Pleas to try trespass and its numerous derivative actions, and so the two courts became in practice, in matters of private law, parallel courts of exactly co-ordinate jurisdiction, and thus they were destined to remain until the Judicature Act 1873. The Bill of Middlesex, which had first robbed Common Pleas of work, and subsequently restored that work sevenfold, survived as a formality until 1832, when it was swept away by the Uniformity of Process Act.

But the activities of King's Bench were by no means bounded by the jurisdiction, extensive as it was, comprised in trespass and its offshoots, and the actions acquired from Common Pleas. Of the breadth in theory, and narrowness in practice, of its criminal jurisdiction, we have already spoken. We must now glance at two other matters of great importance, the prerogative writs and the appellate jurisdication of the court.

The prerogative writs served as the mortar without which the judicial bricks, however strong, could not gain cohesion. We have already discussed *quo warranto*, whereby Edward I overhauled franchise jurisdictions, and which enabled him to destroy those which could not point to a valid basis for their existence. The few remaining franchises were those which, like the Court of Chancery of the County Palatine of Lancaster, the Liverpool Court of Passage, and the Tolzey Court of Bristol, succeeded in satisfying the searching *quo warranto* inquiries, though even they were abolished by the Courts Act 1971. So vigorously were Edward's inquiries prosecuted that the writ had soon served its purpose, but it was recognized that the underlying idea might be utilized for other purposes. In the sixteenth century the place of the writ was taken by *information in the nature of a quo warranto*; which was employed as lately as 1916, when a private individual alleged that a certain person acting as a Privy Councillor had not been validly appointed. It has now, under the Administration of Justice Act 1938, been superseded by the equitable procedure of injunction, which will be discussed later.

Certiorari and prohibition were two writs whereby the court prevented lower courts, and courts of special jurisdiction, from exceeding their proper functions. They are of the highest importance in legal history. Certiorari owes its name to the idea that the king desires to be certified of what is going on in a court. It directs that the issue be brought before the King's Bench. Prohibition, as the name implies, orders the immediate cessation of the trial of an action in the lower court to which it is directed. The former writ is appropriate when the usurpation of jurisdiction is a *fait accompli*, the latter when it has not yet taken place, but is merely proposed, as when a court martial has been assembled for the trial of a person not in fact subject to military law.

The purpose of mandamus was to enable the court to compel an inferior court, or an individual, to perform some act falling within their duty. Thus in the first half of the nineteenth century, when the powers of justices of the peace reached their zenith, a mandamus was granted in the famous case of *R.* v. *Justices of Kent* in 1811, to constrain the justices to hear an application by certain journeymen millers for the fixing of their wages. But this writ has never loomed so large in legal history as certiorari and prohibition, for it was granted only in the absence of a more convenient remedy, though in recent years much greater use has been made of its successor, the order for mandamus.

All three of these writs were abolished by the Administration of Justice Act 1938, which replaced them by *orders* respectively for certiorari, prohibition, and mandamus. These, while assuming the entire character and scope of the old writs, enjoyed the blessings of a simpler procedure, which has been even further simplified with effect from 1978. Rules of courts now provide that under cover of a general application for judicial review the High Court may grant certiorari, prohibition, mandamus, injunction, a declaration, damages, or any combination of these remedies, at its discretion. Certain earlier statutory obstacles to the exercise of certiorari and mandamus were also removed by section 11 of the Tribunals and Inquiries Act 1958 (now replaced by section 14 of the Tribunals and Inquiries Act 1971).

But of even more vital importance is *habeas corpus*. This great writ had a very modest origin, being directed merely to ensuring the due attendance of parties and witnesses before a court, but it was destined to become the bulwark of the liberty of the subject, and the procedure for cases concerning the writ was modernized by the Administration of Justice Act 1960, a statute which also made more ample provision for appeals in such cases direct to the House of Lords. The feature of the British Constitution, evolving from its English origins, which most frequently provides a target for the envy of less happy lands is the impracticability of the *lettre de cachet*. There are countries in which it appears normal and natural that those who fall foul of the executive suffer an arbitrary arrest, and simply disappear, for a protracted period or for ever. But this is one of the things that literally 'cannot happen here'. A deprivation of liberty, without legal justification, constitutes the tort of false imprisonment, and is actionable as a trespass to the person; and the victim will recover heavy damages against anyone whose responsibility he can prove, be he ordinary citizen, policeman, or Secretary of State. But, as Dicey has pointed out, it is of little use for a person in unlawful durance merely to know that an action of false imprisonment is open to him as soon as he can regain his freedom. His gaoler, who shares his knowledge, is all the more likely to prevent his escape. His avenue to freedom is opened by the writ of habeas corpus. A prisoner will indeed be friendless if he cannot find someone to set the machinery of this writ in motion on his behalf. Or he can write to the court; and it has been proved and made very clear that an officious civil servant whose misguided zeal leads him to intercept such a letter commits thereby a very serious contempt of court. It is obligatory for the court in term, or the vacation judge in vacation, to grant the writ, which it will issue to anyone who holds the complainant in captivity.[5] That person must make a 'return', an answer to the writ, which may prove sufficient. For instance, the Governor of Dartmoor would have a clear and complete return in the case of a prisoner duly convicted. Again, the complainant may be a mental patient, or a child in the custody of its legal guardians, or he may have been committed for contempt of one of the Houses of Parliament, whose appropriate officer makes a return to that effect. But if there is anything wrong with the confinement, the court will unhesitatingly order immediate release.

To all these writs we shall have occasion to return before our narrative is ended. It is worthy of mention that, in the seventeenth century, Common Pleas acquired the power to issue two of the prerogative writs, habeas corpus and prohibition; and *Re Hastings* (*No. 3*) in 1959 reminded us that Chancery also shared this power, which was recognized by the Habeas Corpus Act 1679.

Of the appellate jurisdiction of the court it will not be necessary to say more than a few words, as it was destined to be eclipsed on the civil side by the Court of Exchequer Chamber, whose functions

---

[5] But the writ is not ordinarily granted to a person serving a sentence passed by a judge: there must be reason to suspect some irregularity.

are now discharged by the Court of Appeal. The idea of a higher court rehearing a case already tried by a lower court is one that establishes itself only by slow and painful steps in a system of jurisprudence. In Roman Law it is not until the time of Justinian that we find a hierarchy of tribunals; the only expedient open to a disappointed litigant was to sue the judge on the quasi-delict of 'having made the cause his own'. The early English system exhibited less crudity but more complexity. Some American States have preserved in the titles of their appellate courts the word 'error', which raises direful memories in the minds of legal historians.[6] For the writ of error, whereby errors of itinerant justices in criminal matters, or Common Pleas in civil matters, or local courts in either, could be brought up for consideration by the King's Bench, did little to meet practical needs. For it was capricious in its operation, as it was incapable of distinct formulation unless the error complained of appeared on the formal record of the trial. Errors not on the record were irrelevant until the Statute of Westminster II in 1285 provided that a party to a civil action might embody such an error in a writing known as a Bill of Exceptions, and require the judge to seal it; it would then rank as an error on the record. In criminal matters there were alternatives to the writ. A new trial was possible after a conviction for misdemeanour. The year 1848 saw the establishment of the Court for Crown Cases Reserved, wherein questions of law arising at a trial could be determined. The Act of 1907, which launched into our system the Court of Criminal Appeal (replaced in 1966 by the criminal division of the Court of Appeal), abolished the Court for Crown Cases Reserved[7] and the writ of error in criminal cases. The writ of error in civil cases had already been destroyed by the Judicature Act 1873.

---

[6] Thus the highest court in Connecticut is called the Supreme Court of Errors.

[7] This is an elliptical way of expressing the matter. What actually happened was that the jurisdiction of the Court for Crown Cases Reserved, having been transferred by sect. 47 of the Judicature Act 1873 to the Judges of the High Court, was by sect. 20 (4) of the Criminal Appeal Act 1907 vested in the Court of Criminal Appeal.

6 The courts of common law and their several functions – 2

Four things will form the subject-matter of this chapter. First, the time has now arrived for describing in some detail the work of the itinerant justices, who have already been mentioned several times in the course of this narrative. Secondly, we must turn to the third of the common law courts, the Court of Exchequer. Thirdly, we must supplement our account of the appellate jurisdiction of the King's Bench by a delineation of the Court of Exchequer Chamber, by whose powers that jurisdiction was overshadowed and finally superseded. Fourthly, our attention will be claimed by trial by jury.

The itinerant justices fall into two categories, the justices in eyre and the justices of assize. The peregrinations of the former provided, as we have seen, the earliest machinery for securing the control of the central over the local administrations; they were the ancestors of the district auditors, and many other myrmidons of modern officialdom. The work of the eyre was partly judicial, but its main purpose was the conduct of a rigid and minute investigation into every nook and cranny of local administration since the preceding eyre. The sheriff, coroner, reeves, and all local officials were perforce in attendance throughout the eyre. The justices were in the position of inexorable dentists, armed with powerful X-ray apparatus and all the impedimenta of extraction, quartered in the houses of their victims, who were summoned singly or collectively to their dread presence, with no power of appeal from their decisions. They obtained their knowledge of the facts from answers rendered to a questionnaire based on the Articles of the Eyre by a presenting jury of twelve inhabitants of the county, chosen by an elaborate system of indirect election and elimination from nominees of the various hundreds. The most trifling omissions that a searching inquisition could disclose were punished by the infliction of heavy fines. But the career of the eyre was like that of a meteor. It was not destined to longevity. Its judicial work was done more expeditiously by the justices of assize, and its administrative processes gave way to less cumbersome machinery provided by a Parliament which ever waxed in stature and activity. Eyres ceased during the first half of the fourteenth century.

The justices of assize, though their origins were more humble, have enjoyed the more enviable fate of a continuous history until all assize courts were abolished by the Courts Act 1971. With the word 'assize' a loose habit of nomenclature has played havoc. Etymologically, it means no more than a sitting. But it has spread out tentacles, which have embraced a type of action and a type of court. We have already mentioned the grand assize and the possessory assizes, and they will recur in our narrative, for they are important landmarks in the history of trial by jury. This sense of the word is, however, highly technical, and is known only to legal historians.

The whole ceremonial attending the visit of the king's justices to the county towns to try local criminals was redolent of tradition. They radiated from London all over England in unbroken succession beginning in the days of Henry I. We have seen how Henry II reserved all serious crime for the cognizance of the Curia Regis. From being the virtual ruler *of* a county, the sheriff became the chief royal official *in* the county. His function was no longer to try serious crime, but to empanel a jury to 'present' criminals for trial by those projections of the Curia Regis, the royal commissioners of 'oyer and terminer' and 'general gaol delivery'. Statutes of 1272 and 1330 ensured that every county should have regular visitations, by laying down that the circuits of the justices of assize were to take place three times a year, and more often if necessary. Thus the province of the sheriff's tourn became confined to petty crime, until eventually, as we have seen, even this residuum was lost by him to the justices of the peace, and the tourn perished from inanition. The division of crimes into felonies and misdemeanours[1] was supplemented by the more practical division into the indictable, where the accused had always the right to trial by jury, and the non-indictable, which were disposed of summarily by magistrates without a jury.

[1] This classification of crimes was abolished by the Criminal Law Act 1967.

We shall see that, while the courts of the justices of the peace encroached upon the sphere of indictable crime, certain crimes remained always beyond their reach. But the jurisdiction of the assizes in indictable crimes was unlimited. Yet we must not forget that, though the exercise of criminal jurisdiction became in practice almost entirely decentralized, and shared between the assizes and justices of the peace, the King's Bench never dreamed of abandoning its position as a criminal court. It could try a case stated for it by justices of the peace, or review their proceedings by the issue of a writ of certiorari. It also exercised original criminal jurisdiction in several special cases, and in general, where certiorari had been used to remove into it a case wherein an indictment had already been found at the assizes. This process was pernicious, in that it was open to anyone who could afford to pay for it; for, though the judicial level in England is fortunately so high that the advantages of such a change in the scene of trial were for the most part illusory, yet the semblance of difference before the law between rich and poor is as invidious as the reality. Thus it was well that the Administration of Justice Act 1938 contained a provision which all but extinguished the original criminal jurisdiction of the King's Bench Division of the High Court. This process of reform was concluded in 1971.

Although the assize system had lasted for many centuries, dissatisfaction was apparent in recent decades with certain delays in criminal justice, and with the fact that assizes did not always take place in the most convenient urban centres. Eventually the Courts Act 1971 established a more expeditious and overtly acceptable system of criminal courts, the Crown Courts. The Criminal Justice Administration Act 1956 had set up Crown Courts for Manchester and Liverpool only, but these special Crown Courts were abolished by the 1971 Act, along with all assizes and Quarter Sessions, which will be referred to again in Chapter 8. Today all criminal trial on indictment takes place before a judge and jury in the new Crown Courts set up by the 1971 Act. These courts sit in fixed centres throughout England and Wales, and they are grouped into six circuits centred on Birmingham, Leeds, Manchester, London, Cardiff, and Bristol. The judges in each circuit are High Court judges, Circuit Judges, and Recorders, of whom the latter are practising members of the Bar acting as judges on a part-time basis. Magistrates may also sit with a judge in some trials. One or two High Court judges are appointed to act as Presiding Judges for each circuit.

The foolishness of sending coals to Newcastle is proverbial. The assize commissioners for London—which was at an early period made by charter a county—had their work in London, and did not leave it to try London criminals. They included always the Lord Mayor, Recorder and Aldermen of the City of London, and in practice tried all prisoners from London and Middlesex. In 1834 was created the Central Criminal Court, which sat at the Old Bailey, and was in every respect an assize court for what is now Greater London, except that its jurisdiction was entirely over criminal cases. The Courts Act 1971 preserves the name Central Criminal Court for the Crown Court in London, though the non-lawyer judges in practice no longer sit there.

When John Browdie called Mr. Squeers a rascal, Mr. Squeers made a note of it in his pocket-book, and expressed the opinion that the remark would be 'worth full twenty pound at the next assizes'. The question naturally suggests itself, was not Squeers indulging in what is now known as 'wishful thinking'? If he intended to sue John Browdie for slander would he not have had to go to the King's Bench in London? But Squeers was right, for the assizes had civil jurisdiction, under the *'nisi prius'* system. The judge who doffed the red robe, the terror to evil-doers, and donned a black gown for the trial of a civil case, was acting under a provision of that fertile enactment, the Statute of Westminster II of 1285, which was passed in order to counteract a tendency to congestion of business in the Common Pleas and the King's Bench. It gave a general jurisdiction to the justices of assize over all civil cases begun in either of those courts. The machinery for getting a case tried at assizes took the form of a direction to the sheriff to summon the jury to Westminster 'unless first' the justices of assize came into the county. Thus a man could obtain civil justice locally. Later, the system was extended to cover civil cases begun in the Exchequer, which still remain to be discussed. But the Courts Act 1971 not only replaced assizes by Crown Courts exercising solely criminal jurisdiction. It also provided that sittings of the High Court, which will be discussed in Chapter 8, may take place anywhere in England and Wales for the trial of civil cases. Thus the trial of the more serious criminal and civil cases now takes place locally, but in different courts.

The Exchequer was, as we have seen, the financial, as the Chancery was the secretarial, department of State, and the Treasurer was, next to the Justiciar and Chancellor, the greatest and oldest minister of the Crown. Associated with him we find officials known as Barons, a title which has nothing to do with the peerage, and, from 1248 onwards, the Chancellor of the Exchequer, who before that date was merely the Chancellor's clerk, and whose change of name carried with it a great access of dignity and importance. The bias towards differentiation of functions which forms so marked a feature of the late thirteenth century carried the judicial work of the Exchequer to a certain distance from its purely administrative work, and the Barons gradually came to be recruited entirely from lawyers.

The court was, first and foremost, a court of revenue. It decided questions at issue between the Crown on the one hand, and on the other the taxpayer, and the accountants of the Crown, that is to say those officials, such as sheriffs, whose duty might involve the collection of money on behalf of the Crown. The special procedure used in such cases was known as the '*cursus scaccarii*'.[2] But the Exchequer was not content with its position as a court of special and exclusive financial jurisdiction. It took a leaf out of the book of King's Bench by the use of a fiction in order to appropriate jurisdiction over common pleas. The tool it employed to render itself a common law tribunal was borrowed from the armoury of implements wherewith it protected the monetary interests of the Crown. It was known as the writ of *Quominus*, a word painfully familiar to every student of the elements of Latin prose composition. The court was even bolder than King's Bench, in that it had to deflect positive prohibitions, imposed by statutes and ordinances of the thirteenth century, against its hearing common pleas. It achieved its object by an allegation that the plaintiff, in a case which it desired to appropriate, was an accountant of the Crown, that is to say owed money to the Crown, and that the defendant would not pay him his debt, 'by which the less' the plaintiff was able to discharge his debt to the Crown. This fiction

[2] 'Course of the Exchequer.'

was left untouched by the Statute of 1661 which, as we have seen, temporarily balked King's Bench in its path of spoliation, and by its nature defied any reprisals by Common Pleas, which, not being concerned with revenue matters, was not competent to use it. It was abolished, together with the Bill of Middlesex, by the Uniformity of Process Act 1832.

The court had also a third and, in some ways, most interesting aspect. It was a court of equity, and thus straddled the gulf between the common law courts and the Court of Chancery. The discussion of this side of its jurisdiction will be postponed until we come to speak at length of that more important court of equity, the Court of Chancery. It was not until 1842 that the equitable jurisdiction of the Exchequer was merged in that of the Court of Chancery.

The time approaches for discussing the Court of Exchequer Chamber, and our account of this court, or rather these courts, for there were two,[3] created at times two centuries distant from one another, must be preceded by a short recapitulation of the system of appeals. We have seen that 'system' is really the wrong word to use, as the principles on which superior courts could supervise and overhaul the proceedings of inferior courts were never planned but, like so many things in English history, were allowed to grow up haphazard. It is not even correct to talk, in this connexion, of superior and inferior courts, for King's Bench had an unquestionable jurisdiction to hear appeals brought by writ of error from Common Pleas, whose lawyers would have died in the last ditch rather than admit any sort of inferiority. King's Bench laid claim to a similar appellate jurisdiction from decisions of the Exchequer, but the Barons strenuously resisted, and in 1338 they addressed a reasoned statement to the Crown, demonstrating the lack of any historical basis for the claim. As a result of this, the earlier of the two Courts of Exchequer Chamber was established by a statute of 1357–8, to hear appeals from Exchequer. The wording of the statute is peculiar, for it mentions as necessary judges of the court, only the Chancellor and Treasurer, giving power to them, however, to co-opt 'the justices and other sage persons such as to them seemeth to be taken'. In 1668, a vacancy in the office of

---

[3] The name was also given to certain other tribunals.

Treasurer necessitated the passage of further legislation on this matter, and this Act, instead of associating other judges with the Chancellor, simply reduced the effective personnel of the court from two to one. Judgment could be given by the Chancellor alone. The Barons, if they sat with him, gave their opinions on sufferance only. Their position was like that of members of a committee wherein only the chairman had a vote, or, to take a rather daring analogy, of the members of the President's Cabinet in the United States. A familiar story is told of Lincoln, who put a question to his Cabinet, and found them unanimously of the negative opinion, which happened to disagree with his own. 'The Ayes have it' was Lincoln's bold and quite constitutional decision. The omnipotence of the Chancellor in the Court was shown by the course taken by the famous *Bankers' Case*. Charles II was, apart from the revenues from Crown lands, ostensibly in a position of complete financial dependence on Parliament. This being so, it is at first sight a matter for surprise that he should have been able to dispense with any Parliament at all during the last few years of his reign. The secret Treaty of Dover had rendered Louis XIV to a certain, but not to a sufficient, extent his almoner. The balance of his requirements he made up by negotiating large loans from the Bankers on the security of the public revenue. In 1696, when the financial supremacy of the Commons had been fully established and annual sessions of Parliament became the order of the day, the Bankers sought recovery of their money. The Exchequer having decided the case in favour of the claim of the Bankers, the Crown appealed to Exchequer Chamber, where all the judges, except Treby, the Chief Justice of Common Pleas, agreed with the judgment. Lord Keeper Somers, however, in an elaborate and highly technical judgment, enunciated the contrary opinion, and the judges acquiesced in the interpretation of the statutes of 1357 and 1668 which allowed him to be a triumphant majority of one. The judgment of the Exchequer was accordingly reversed, only to be restored by the House of Lords.

We have already discussed the position of the House of Lords as a court of law in connexion with the doctrine of the separation of powers. We have seen that, though its claim to act as a court of original civil jurisdiction was disputed by the Commons, and ultimately abandoned, its appellate jurisdiction from the common law courts was never seriously challenged. So it was the final court which heard appeals from Exchequer, King's Bench, and, at one remove, from Common Pleas. Cases at first reached the House of Lords by petition, but from the reign of Edward IV onwards the writ of error, with all its imperfections, came to be generally used. But the drawback to the House of Lords lay in the fact that, prior to the Revolution of 1688, years might pass without the assembly of Parliament, and so appeals pending from King's Bench languished unheard. The reproach of a void of justice was removed by the establishment, in 1585, of the second, and of course quite distinct, Court of Exchequer Chamber, whose function it was to hear the errors of King's Bench. Its judicial personnel was to consist of the justices of Common Pleas and Barons of the Exchequer, six of these forming a quorum. The House of Lords retained its final appellate powers, being thus placed at two stages' remove from King's Bench as from Exchequer, and at three from Common Pleas. It was not until 1830 that Parliament realized that four stages in the process of an appeal were excessive, and abolished the jurisdiction of King's Bench to amend errors of Common Pleas. It amalgamated the two Courts of Exchequer Chamber, and made the composite court into a court of appeal intermediate between all three common law courts and the final jurisdiction of the House of Lords. The work of the three courts had by then become virtually identical, and little but sentiment remained to delay their complete union, whose desirability was obvious. But the delay was beneficial, for the consummation finally achieved in 1873 was far more comprehensive. It went far beyond the mere unification of common law jurisdiction; it united with the common law courts the Court of Chancery, which administered equity.

We must now turn to the mainspring of common law procedure, trial by jury. To common law procedure it was indeed confined; at no time was it known to Star Chamber or to Chancery. But in cases coming before the courts of Common Law, and more especially in criminal trials before the itinerant justices, it became more than a bulwark against injustice. Few people today would claim that a British jury is infallible, but since the inception of the jury system it has been widely agreed that before any person is convicted of a serious crime it is a valuable safeguard to liberty that twelve ordinary citizens, rather than just one professional judge, should be satisfied of his guilt. Legal literature from Fortescue's *De Laudibus Legum Angliae*,[4] in the latter part of the fifteenth century, to Stephen's *History of the Criminal Law* in the middle of the nineteenth, tends to institute comparisons between our system of trial by jury and the inquisitory procedure in vogue in Continental countries, which came to them as a legacy from Roman Law. It is only in the detachment and disillusionment of quite modern times that we have abandoned the exuberant and complacent assumption that every institution of our own system is necessarily better than the corresponding institution in the systems of our neighbours, and that their laws are tolerable only in so far as they coincide with our own. The stern logic of events is implanting in our minds the realization that a drab uniformity of system is incompatible with diversities of race and temperament; that a rule or a process which is to one people as natural as the breath of life, is to another people repugnant and incomprehensible. Some European countries have in modern times made an experiment of the jury system, only to abandon it as unsuitable.

History is a freakish thing, and its offspring often belie their early promise. In Bernard Shaw's *John Bull's Other Island* Larry Doyle, on being reproached by Nora for showing excessive devotion to England by singing 'Tell England I'll forget her never', replied, 'Oh that was written by a German Jew, like most patriotic English sentiment.' This statement is the expression of more than mere Shavian cynicism. It has been a besetting sin in England to borrow a thing from abroad, and then to grow so attached to the thing borrowed as to forget the very fact of the loan. Trial by jury was brought to us by our Norman kings, who had learned it from the French kings of whom, though in antipathy and contempt, they held their lands. The root from which it sprang was the practice of the Carolingian monarchs, adopted by their Capetian successors, of summoning the members of a community, and making them supply any desired information. This was the plan of William I in the compilation of the survey on which Domesday Book was based. Under the able hands of Henry II the shapeless dough was kneaded, until it emerged as the loaf of a system for the determination of issues of fact. He used it for the purpose of assessing taxes.

---

[4] Written for the instruction of Prince Edward, the son of Henry VI.

Instead of demanding arbitrary sums, he would in effect take the sworn opinion of a man's neighbours as to the limits of his capacity to pay. He used it for the trial of crime. It was, as we have seen, part and parcel of the method of indictment, which under his encouragement gradually superseded the method of appeal, which was tried by battle. He dealt another staggering blow to trial by battle by his institution of the Grand Assize in actions for the recovery of land. Later, throughout the whole field of civil litigation, the fairy weapon of trespass enabled the jury system to win victory after victory over its predecessors. The older methods were so unsatisfactory, and their defects so palpable, that it is matter for wonder that two of them, battle and compurgation, should have lasted, even as attenuated ghosts, until the nineteenth century. It can be explained only by reminding ourselves that English sentiment has at all periods of history hesitated to put old friends, though senile in their debility, out of their pain. The production of *secta*, which has already been described as an indispensable stage in the process of the older methods of trial, had no rational application to the jury system, and yet it survived as an empty form until 1852.

It was in part the very weakness of its older rivals that served to demonstrate the vitality of the jury system, which rapidly grew in stature. Rejected by France, the country of its origin, it found a permanent home in England; and when, in quite modern times, it revisited France, it came in the guise of an adaptation from the other side of the Channel.

What is the function of the jury? The easy answer is, to determine issues of fact. But two other queries are not susceptible of so easy a solution. Where does law end and fact begin? And how are the respective spheres of activity of judge and jury to be demarcated? A medieval maxim of uncertain origin runs, '*ad quaestionem facti non respondent iudices; ita ad quaestionem iuris non respondent iuratores*'.[5] But this is a half-truth. It is indeed no part of the business of the jury to decide matters of law, yet without receiving a thorough explanation of the legal principles bearing on a case they cannot form a right judgment on the facts. A jury must decide whether A met his death at the hands of B; they must further

[5] 'To a question of fact the judges do not answer; so to a question of law the jurors do not answer.'

decide whether B's act amounted to murder or to manslaughter; the first question they can determine according to their intelligence, but the latter they can never answer unless the judge thoroughly explains, over and over again if need be, the precise significance of that mystical 'malice aforethought', which forms the dividing line between the greater crime and the less. Ownership is a matter of law, possession of mixed law and fact, detention of pure fact. An infant is not liable to pay for goods sold to him unless they are necessaries; the question whether goods fall within this category is primarily one of law for the judge, in the sense that if they are such that on no conceivable hypothesis can they be considered as necessaries, the judge must forthwith 'non-suit' the tradesman plaintiff, that is to say, decide the case in favour of the infant defendant without having submitted it to the jury at all; but if he comes to the conclusion that they can reasonably be considered as necessaries he must leave the question for the jury, if a jury is sitting in the case, stressing that they must direct their minds to two points, the suitability of the goods to the infant's position in life, and his actual requirements at the time of the contract of sale. Sometimes the legislature has turned a question of law into a question of fact, for instance Fox's Law of Libel Act 1792 transferred the determination of the crucial question 'libel or no libel' from the arbitrament of the judge to that of the jury. Sometimes a finding of fact is allowed to masquerade for a period as an enunciation of a principle of law, until directed back to its proper place by the House of Lords or Court of Appeal; e.g. the latter court during the 1939–45 war took occasion to remark that a judge in emphasizing the need for greater caution in black-out conditions is talking in terms of fact, not of law. Finally, it is quite untrue that the judge has nothing to do with the facts. On the contrary, in his summing-up he must collect all the facts as revealed by the evidence, turn the case, in Dickens's phrase, 'now inside-out, now outside-in', evaluate the relative importance of each item, and hint to the jury which witnesses are unworthy of credence.

These points are taken, almost at random, from among the many which float across the mental vision of a writer engaged in attempting to convey a picture of the mutual relations of judge and jury, a subject which, if treated fully, would occupy a large volume. From the *functions* of the jury we must pass to their *character*. This has passed through two well-defined phases. They were at first regarded as witnesses, who could speak of their own expert knowledge, either of relevant technicalities, or of the facts themselves. This view melted before the advance of the rules of evidence. Technical matters would pass through the filter of the expert witness before reaching the jury, and in general the jury would be told to decide the issue of fact, not according to their own knowledge of the circumstances or preconceived ideas, but entirely on the basis of the testimony presented to them, at the hearing of the case in court, by witnesses in the course of interrogation by the counsel for the parties, and sifted for their examination by the judge in his summing-up. In other words, juries ceased to be witnesses, and became judges of the facts. Originally the verdict of a majority carried the day, but in 1357 the rule of unanimity was adopted, and it was not until the Criminal Justice Act 1967 that the position was reversed again. Now a majority verdict is acceptable, provided that the jury has deliberated for not less than two hours, and that the minority is not more than two in number (or one, if the jury has been reduced, e.g. by illness, to eleven or ten). The effect of this measure is intended to neutralize the occasional perverse juror, and largely to eliminate any injustice worked by a corrupted or intimidated juror. The Criminal Justice Acts of 1967 and 1972 also widened and brought up to date the legal qualifications for jury service, so that today they accord very nearly to the qualifications for entry on the electoral roll (i.e. citizens of full age), save that certain persons are ineligible (such as judges and lawyers), others are disqualified (after criminal conviction), and some may be excused if they so wish (such as doctors, M.P.s, members of the Scottish Assembly, if it comes into being, representatives to the Assembly of the European Community, and members of the armed forces). Most of the modern law on juries and jury service is now consolidated in the Juries Act 1974, but the payment of expenses and allowances to jurors is regulated by the Administration of Justice Act 1977.

The mark which chiefly distinguishes indictable from non-indictable crime is the right of one accused of the former to demand trial by jury. It may be demanded also for the trial of certain tort cases, but in modern times the importance of trial by jury, constant as a rock in criminal cases, is, in civil cases, with the growing complexity of commercial litigation, receding, and whether the case be criminal or civil we have now no classification of juries, for 'special juries', which could be got for payment, have now been abolished. But historically we must distinguish criminal from civil juries. Among the latter we have already noticed the grand assize, and the three possessory assizes of novel disseisin, darrein presentment, and mort d'ancestor, which form in a sense a bridge between the writ of right and the action of ejectment to which it gave place. We must also notice the assize *utrum*, empanelled to decide the question whether a piece of land was held by frankalmoign or by one of the lay tenures, and the jurata, who might be summoned to decide incidental questions of fact, over and above those put to the assize. The elliptical phrase of Bracton, *'assisa vertitur in juratam'*,[6] signified simply that the need for deciding additional facts called for the meeting of a further body of persons to determine them. Criminal juries were of two varieties, the grand jury and the petty jury. Another and more descriptive name for the former was the jury of presentment, summoned by the sheriff, in his character of chief royal official in the county, to present prisoners awaiting trial to the itinerant justices. The number summoned by him was twenty-four; from these twenty-three were chosen, and their duty was simply to decide whether, on the evidence of the prosecution, which alone they heard, there was a case to go for trial. If the majority opinion was in the affirmative, the jury would 'return a true bill'; if in the negative, they would 'ignore'. In the former case a new jury, called the petty jury, which was destined to become the only real, live jury, would be empanelled, to hear both sides and try the issue of fact. By a statute of 1351 it was laid down that no member of a grand jury could sit on a petty jury if 'challenged' for this cause by the accused. Gradually the grand jury passed from a reality to a formality, and from a formality to a redundancy, for the growth of the powers of the justices of the peace provided a far more efficient method of preliminary investigation. When justices had heard evidence on both sides, there was no need for a grand jury to be interposed, to hear one side only, between the justices and the petty jury. But though logic urged the abolition of the grand jury, sentiment demanded its retention,

---

[6] 'The assize is turned into a jurata.'

praying in aid arguments which already cause us to smile, such as the value of membership of the grand jury to the legal education of the country gentry. Grand juries were suspended in 1917, but revived six months after the end of the 1914–18 war. They were finally abolished by sect. 31 (3) of the Criminal Justice Act 1948.

A candid historian cannot pretend that our criminal law and procedure has been at all times humane. Torture was, except in one particular, the monopoly of the Court of Star Chamber, but one form of torture was well known at common law. It arose out of the rule that a prisoner could not be tried by a jury without his consent. If, therefore, an accused person would not plead, but elected to 'stand mute', the trial could not proceed. But the law would not suffer itself to be thus baffled without a terrible struggle. A statute of 1275 authorized the use of the 'peine forte et dure' to extort consent. This consisted in pressing the accused beneath heavy weights until he consented or died.[7] The reason why persons would choose to suffer these appalling agonies rather than plead was that thus they would avoid the forfeiture of property which would, until its abolition in 1870, follow a conviction for treason or felony. In 1772 the barbarity that had so long disfigured the law was ended by an enactment that standing mute in cases of felony should be equivalent to a conviction. In 1827 the law was again altered, and it was provided that, if the prisoner, in any criminal case, stands mute, a plea of not guilty shall be entered, and the trial shall proceed as if he had thus pleaded.

Conceding that British juries generally reach the correct conclusion, we must yet admit that sometimes they arrive at the wrong one. In nine cases out of ten they do so owing to a misdirection by the judge, which may form the subject-matter of an appeal. But supposing their error to be deliberate and perverse, is there any means of punishing them? Not now,[8] but once they were liable to

---

[7] We are reminded that the process was carried to America by the Pilgrim Fathers, by Longfellow's macabre tragedy *Giles Cory of the Salem Farms*. More recently, Clemence Dane, in her novel *Regiment of Women*, has harrowed our feelings most effectively by purporting to convey its stark horror through the medium of a schoolgirl's essay.

[8] Unless their conduct amounts to an act of *embracery*, which postulates actual corruption. This is, however, more likely to be committed by someone trying to influence a juror than by the juror himself, and it is likely to be dealt with as a contempt of court.

punishment through the jurisdiction of the Court of Star Chamber, and through the writ of attaint. The power of the Star Chamber to amerce a jury for a false or corrupt verdict perished in 1641 with the court itself, but the writ of attaint is an historical curiosity demanding a brief description, which must be modelled on the lucid account given by Fortescue. We first hear of it at the beginning of the thirteenth century, and it was extended, by a statute of 1360, to all actions real and personal. Fortescue tells us that a party aggrieved by a verdict could sue out the writ against both the jury who recorded it and the party who obtained it. 'An *attaint jury* of twenty-four was then empanelled, and a finding by them that the verdict was contrary to the evidence and the jury's oath, rendered the first jury liable to very severe penalties, including imprisonment, forfeiture of property, and perpetual infamy. A successful attaint would also involve the reversal of the verdict. His careful use of the word 'parties' suggests that it was applicable only to the verdicts of civil juries. As a matter of fact it was not until 1670, in *Bushell's Case*, that it was conclusively laid down that a jury could not be fined or imprisoned for failing to find any verdict in a criminal trial which the judge had directed them to find. This virtually spelt the end of the writ of attaint, though *Bushell's Case* itself concerned not attaint, but the imprisonment of jurors for contempt of court. Not the least part of the shameless injustice of Lord Jeffreys in the trial of Lady Alice Lisle for treason sixteen years later was that he coerced them into a verdict of guilty by the threat of attaint which he knew to be vain.

The procedure survived in civil cases until its formal abolition in 1825, but, as Holdsworth has pointed out, it became an anachronism as soon as juries entirely lost their old character of witnesses, and assumed their modern character of judges of the facts. Nowadays perverse findings by juries are happily rare; if they occur, judges may comment on their conduct, though it is probably wiser to refrain from comment, but they can in no way be punished. In *Reg.* v. *McKenna* in 1960, it was even held that a judge may not hurry a jury into arriving at their verdict. On the other hand, the Criminal Appeal Act 1966 allows the verdict of a jury to be set aside on appeal if, even in the absence of any misdirection by the judge, it is unsafe or unsatisfactory having regard to all the circumstances of the case.

It must not be thought that juries have ever been universally obligatory in the courts. In the Chancery and the Star Chamber they were unknown. Petty crime has for centuries been tried, for the most part, by magistrates. In the case of indictable crime adults have always a right, which very often they do not exercise, to demand trial by jury. In actions for damages for tort and breach of contract, juries are nowadays the exception rather than the rule, for, except in cases of defamation and fraud, the judge normally sits without a jury, and himself decides questions both of law and of fact. But the division between these two spheres remains: thus, in an action against an infant to recover the price of goods sold, it is only if the judge is of opinion that the goods can reasonably, as a matter of law, be considered as necessaries, that his functions as judge of fact come into play. It is worth noticing that for serious criminal cases in Northern Ireland trial by jury is the rule, except in times when special emergency provisions come into operation, in which case criminal trials may proceed without a jury. Regrettably, such emergency provisions have had to be invoked during the last few years.

7 The Court of Chancery and the system of equity

We have seen that, after the disappearance of the justiciar in the middle of the thirteenth century, the Chancellor became the most important man in the country after the king. As well as being the chief adviser to the king, and the leading member of his Council, he held the only key to the storehouse of civil procedure. For he who would bring an action in the Curia Regis must first obtain from the Chancellor the appropriate writ. But the Chancellor was destined to be brought into a far more direct proximity to the judicial system than that enjoyed by him as the originator of actions at common law. For events so shaped themselves that he himself became, not merely a judge, but the head of the whole judicial hierarchy. It is the object of this chapter to explain how this state of affairs came about.

Let us recall Maine's estimate, that the three expedients for bringing law into harmony with the needs of society are legal fictions, equity, and legislation. The first have already been discussed; they provide an excellent means of tempering the wind of change to the shorn lamb of tradition; or, to employ a military metaphor, they play the part of camouflage nets, under cover of which the vehicles of legal institutions are modernized. They can, however, have only a local effect. The arm of equity is far longer and more searching.

We are familiar with the phrase, 'hard cases make bad law'. When Portia refused to 'wrest once the law to her authority', she placed her refusal on the sound ground that ''twill be recorded for a precedent; and many errors by the same example will rush into the State.' The same idea has been put in a different way in the aphorism that it is better that the law should be certain, than that it should be ideally just. But at the same time, some cases are so hard that they cry out for relief, a refusal of which would bring the administration of law into contempt. Every legal system has had to face this problem: how, while preserving rigidity in the law, to prevent that rigidity from causing real suffering in individual cases. Few legal systems have succeeded in solving this problem without the aid of equity.

But the mutual relations of law and equity show us a variegated panorama. In Roman Law equity was the inevitable reaction to the exclusiveness of Roman citizenship. Aliens were incapable of the formal ceremonials whereby alone transfers of property and other acts in the law might be effected. Yet they played a considerable part in the world of commerce, and their transactions could not be ignored. So in 242 B.C. was instituted the office of *praetor peregrinus*, who gave to their acts a defined legal status; a transfer of property by mere delivery from an alien would give to the transferee 'bonitary' ownership which would, through uninterrupted possession for a certain period, ripen into the full ownership of the civil law. Thus grew up an ever-expanding volume of equity, under the name of *jus gentium*, the law common to all nations, in so far as this could be visualized in the edict of the peregrine praetor. In Scotland, the Court of Sessions may, by virtue of the *nobile officium* inherent in it, turn itself into a court of equity for hard cases in which the law gives no remedy.

The Roman and Scottish systems are alike in this, that law and equity were administered by the same court. In the time of Justinian, we find that *jus gentium* has swallowed up the civil law, and this is the reason why French Law, which grew up under the shadow of the developed Roman tradition, has never felt the need for equity. But the English system, peculiar in other features, is peculiar also in this. For equity was evolved mainly by courts distinct from those of the common law, and this duality of tribunals persisted until the Judicature Act 1873. It was commonly said of this Act, in the late nineteenth and early twentieth centuries, that it fused together, not the systems of law and equity themselves, but merely the courts in which they had been severally administered. It seemed that the two systems differed so widely in procedure, in technique, in the qualities demanded of their respective practitioners, that they must defy all attempts at amalgamation. But the Act is now over a century old, and judges are so familiar with the necessity to take into account, in the decision of a case, legal and equitable doctrine alike, that we may now rationally speak of a fusion of the systems.

In what did equitable procedure differ from the procedure of the common law courts? We have seen that at the root of the common law system lay the principle of the royal writs. He who sought legal redress must choose the writ appropriate to this cause of action. A choice of trespass where case should have been brought, or of case where assumpsit should have been brought, was fatal to the plaintiff's success. The flow of the river of justice was clogged by the entangling reeds of process. Furthermore, the writ must be correctly drawn. It must state the exact matter which the defendant was to be called upon to answer. Clearly many cases, wherein the plaintiff had on his side the entirety of abstract right, fell right outside the ambit of any common law writ. And technicality was not the only danger a litigant had to face. For his case might fall within the compass of a writ, and yet he would perhaps lose it through the intimidation or corruption of a jury, against which the social conditions of the Middle Ages afforded no sure talisman. The defects of the common law could be balanced only by a tribunal whose procedure should be more or less free from technical rules, presided over by a judge so exalted as to be unassailable by an unscrupulous defendant, however powerful. Such a judge was found in the Chancellor himself, whose prestige as the second man in the realm, and estimation as a high dignitary of the Church, rested beyond cavil or question. For the earlier Chancellors were not lawyers, but ecclesiastics. They were known as the 'keepers of the king's conscience', and in this capacity they operated the reserve of justice always inherent in the king as the fountain of all justice. Appeals to the Chancellor were couched in humble and piteous terms; a suppliant for relief would implore the Chancellor to right his wrong 'for God and in way of charity'. We now come to the four ways in which the Chancellor's procedure differed fundamentally from that of the common law.

(*a*) The Chancellor proceeded not by writ at all, but by bill. By his weapon of subpoena he would summon the defendant to appear before him to answer not only, as in the common law system of writs, charges named in the bill itself, but other *unspecified* charges as well.

(*b*) In case of contumacy, the Chancellor would order the arrest of the defendant, and his imprisonment for contempt. The rule that 'Equity acts in personam'[1] is the lantern that guides us through the entire labyrinth of equity jurisprudence. A common law court's only resource was to order the payment of damages, followed, in case of non-payment, by a writ of *fieri facias*, or of *elegit*, addressed to the sheriff, empowering him to seize and sell sufficient of the defendant's goods in the one case, and land in the other, to satisfy the judgment. But the courses open to the Chancellor were less monotonous. He could grant specific performance, that is to say, order the defendant to perform a contract according to its terms, or injunction, that is to say, order him to desist from conduct prejudicial to the plaintiff; and, like a skilful fisherman, would never let him go, once hooked, but could always jerk him back to obedience by the threat or fact of personal constraint.

(*c*) Juries were at no time seen in the Court of Chancery, the Chancellor acting as judge both of the law and of the facts.

(*d*) The Chancellor in early times acted entirely according to the dictates of conscience, and on no theory of judicial precedent. He would grant or withhold relief on no criterion other than his own view of the merits of the particular case.

In its inception, therefore, equity was not a system, but simply the name given to the sum of spasmodic decrees issued by the Chancellor in individual cases of hardship, where either common law provided no remedy, or the remedy had proved inadequate or abortive.

We have seen that the Chancery was the secretarial, as the Exchequer was the financial, department of State, and over both hovered the power of the King's Council. During the fourteenth century the judicial functions of the Chancery, with the Chancellor at its head, began to separate themselves from its administrative functions, but at no time does the separation become complete; and while the possession of the Great Seal places the Chancellor on the topmost rung of the judicial ladder, at no time does he lose his connexion with the executive; and this explains why at the present day his work is a medley of administrative and judicial duties, and the nature of his office provides a fourth illustration—along with the preponderance of the executive in the Commons, the dual

---

[1] 'Equity acts *against the person*.'

position of the House of Lords as an Upper Legislative Chamber and a Supreme Law Court, and the executive flavour of the work of the Judicial Committee of the Privy Council—of the absence, in the English Constitution, of any real influence wielded by the doctrine of the separation of powers. *Rex est procurator fatuorum*;[2] so the Chancellor supervises the guardianship of lunatics, and of 'pretty young wards in Chancery'—though wardship powers are now exercised by the Family Divison of the High Court. He presides over all sessions of the House of Lords. He has the appointment to many ecclesiastical benefices. But it is with the Chancellor as a judge that we are here concerned.

Early equity stood in sharp contrast to common law in its freedom from the shackles of judicial precedent. Chancery Reports were unknown until the reign of Mary I. But oral tradition and the routine of practice inevitably shaped a coherent organism. Many a profound truth is contained in a homely rhyme, and the scope of equity jurisdiction was well expressed under the three comprehensive headings of 'fraud, accident, and breach of confidence'. The first two gave the Chancellor a firm foothold in the field of written documents, and especially in that of contract, where the common law gave no remedy unless the agreement were under seal. It was at one time thought that the doctrine of consideration was the child of equity. This attribution of paternity is now disproved; but the medieval Chancery, working along an unfrequented path, would grant relief arbitrarily in cases where no seal had been affixed, but faith had been pledged, on the elementary ground that it was in the interests of fair play that reliance on this faith should not be disappointed.

But it is the third heading under which falls the greatest volume of equity, that gigantic rubric which forms two-thirds of its entire content, the law of trusts. The ancestor of the modern trust was the medieval *use* of land, an institution of which foreign systems never seem to have felt the need. The idea underlying the whole conception baffles the foreign inquirer at once by its very simplicity and by its delusive resemblance to the spirit of his own institutions. The Roman Law, and systems which followed it, were familiar with *fideicommissum*, which obliged one person, at first in honour

[2] 'The king looks after the weak.'

and then in law, to hand over an inheritance, or a portion of it or specified things in it, to another; familiar also with the usufruct, or right of life enjoyment by one person of the property of another. But the use, though exhibiting superficial likenesses to both of these, nevertheless differed fundamentally from both in that its whole conception involved not a relinquishment by one person in favour of another but permanent dominion and stewardship on his behalf. The institution, in common with so many English devices, made an almost imperceptible entry through the back door of utility, and had penetrated right into the inner sanctum of the household of the law before its intrusion had begun to arouse resentment, or even remark.

The first important advertisement for the system was provided by the practical need for some method of obviating the difficulties caused by the position of the Franciscan friars. These were bound by vows of poverty to hold no property, and yet they must have somewhere to live. A simple solution was provided by conveying land to a borough community *to the use of the friars*. Thus was forged an engine that was to prove a dynamic force in the power-house of the legal system. For it came to be realized that it could be used to evade the burdensome incubus of feudal dues, which might, as we have seen, impose a crushing burden on the tenant by knight's service. Prominent among these dues were the lord's rights of wardship and marriage. But the tenant could evade them by simply enfeoffing, that is to say transferring his land to, several persons, to be held by them to his own use, that is to say for his benefit and according to his directions. Wardship and marriage would thus go into abeyance, for a plurality of persons, unless they were husband and wife, could have no one heir, and no daughter. Once started on its career, the use began to emulate the destructive antics of Coppelia. For, having made a dent in feudalism, it proceeded to smash other strongholds of the medieval common law. For that law forbade a tenant, except in certain localities, to make a will of his land. But the use enabled him to ignore this prohibition, by carrying his directions to his feoffees to uses over the time of his own death. The common law could lodge no objection, if B, C, and D chose to employ *their* land for the benefit of E, as directed by the deceased A. But how if the feoffees disregarded those directions and held the land for their own advantage?

It is here that the use presents its most seductive analogy to the Roman *fideicommissum*, in that the same historical sequence was common to both. For the obligation moved from a position in which it bound in honour only to one in which it was vigorously enforced: in the case of the Roman institution, by a special *praetor fideicommissarius*; in the case of the English institution, by the equity of the Court of Chancery, which thus made an immense stride forward towards the centre of the stage of real property law.

Uses sprang into great popularity. To the poorer tenant they spelled a blessed release from intolerable exactions; to the richer tenant, with tenants of his own, they were on the whole acceptable, for his losses as lord were more than compensated by his savings as tenant. But the position of the king was gravely prejudiced, for to him the system brought nothing but loss. On his feudal dues he relied largely for the expenses of government, and as more and more land became exempted from payment of those dues, larger and larger grew the dread spectre of dependence on Parliament for his ordinary, as well as for his extraordinary financial supplies. This monster could not frighten Henry VII, whose frugality kept its advances at bay. But so extravagant was the young Henry VIII, with the Field of the Cloth of Gold and the war with Scotland, that by 1530 it had begun to thunder at his door. A lesser king might have succumbed and accepted the situation, and the exclusive control of the Commons over taxation, and the necessity for their annual assembly which was its corollary, which was underlined by the abolition of military tenures in 1660, and confirmed by the Bill of Rights in 1689, might have been brought about a hundred and fifty years earlier by the oblique effect of the equitable doctrine. But Henry VIII was made of sterner stuff. Part of his financial deficit he made good by the spoliation of the monasteries, but still expenditure overtopped income. So he decided to strike a mortal blow at the rodent which was gnawing with ever greater greed at his revenues, regardless of the fact that the animal was the pet of the most important section of his subjects. By a mixture of cajolery and threats he induced Parliament, in 1535, to agree to the Statute of Uses, which turned the use into the legal estate. That is to say, if A, B, and C held Blackacre to the use of D, the three feoffees were henceforth to have no rights whatever in the land, but became simply the inert lay figures through which the legal estate passed to

D. This statute at one blow replenished the royal coffers and destroyed the power of leaving land by will. But its later history was curious. Within five years Henry VIII found himself forced to agree to the passage of the Statute of Wills, which legalized in large measure a will of land. And the statute never destroyed the equitable estate in land. Avowedly, indeed, it was hostile to the institution only in so far as it was used as a pretence, in order to enable tenants to evade payment of their feudal dues. It was never intended to arrest the action of equity in cases where the feoffees' duties were genuine, where they were directed to collect rents and profits and pay them over to the beneficiary. The passive use of land, however, was for the time being completely destroyed. But only for the time being. For in 1660 military tenures were abolished, and the spectre which haunted the foresight of Henry VIII became a living reality.

The Act of 1660 eliminated feudalism from the field of public law, though in private law, in the law of real property, it continued to play a mischievous part until 1925. After 1660, therefore, there remained no longer a reason for the continued suppression of equitable estates and interests, and they were reinstated under the name of trusts. The method whereby the Court of Chancery achieved their revival is too technical to describe here; nor is it, in the general scheme of things, of great importance, for if we look on English legal history as a whole, we must realize that the separation of legal and equitable estates had become an essential and inevitable part of its framework. It soon became clear that the trust was required to serve more lofty ends than those served by uses. It became of the utmost value in family settlements; married women started on the long road to emancipation from the shackles of the old common law rule which inexorably transferred their entire property into the pockets of their husbands, and it became unthinkable that a woman of any wealth should marry without a settlement which placed the bulk of her capital, whether of land or money, or both, in the hands of trustees, bound by directions to hold it for her separate use. Again, the trust is at the bottom of that conception which plays so vital a part in the legal, commercial, social, and religious life of today, the Unincorporate Body. The Stock Exchange, London Clubs, the Jockey Club, Trades Unions, the Methodists—how do all these hold their property? They are not incorporated, and so are not persons in the eye of the law. The truth is, that if property is to be vested in a body of persons, this must be done either by means of incorporation, or by vesting the whole property in the hands of trustees, on trust to apply it for the benefit of the members of the unincorporate body, though in recent years the courts have come to the point of virtually accepting that Trades Unions, wielding vast industrial power, are indeed legal persons in their own right.

It is important to understand the exact nature of equitable interests in property. They cannot exist apart from the legal ownership of the trustee. Equity will vindicate them not only as against the trustee himself, but as against anyone to whom he may, in breach of trust, transfer the trust property, but subject to one very important exception. For equity will always treat as inviolable a bona-fide purchaser for value, that is to say a person who has purchased the property, and not received it as a present, and furthermore has purchased it in ignorance of the trust by which it was bound.

The use formed the most voluminous part of medieval, as does the trust of modern, equity. But in the period between the suppression of the former and the revival of the latter, equity was by no means idle. For his preoccupation with the integrity of the human conscience impelled the Chancellor to use the weapon of injunction to restrain a litigant from making an unconscientious use of his legal rights. He would be restrained, on grounds whereof the Chancellor claimed particular knowledge, from suing in a common law court, or from proceeding to execution of a judgment obtained in such a court. This practice could hardly fail to arouse the resentment of the common law judges, and a struggle ensued, which came to a head in the reign of James I, with two men of exceptional strength of character and intellect as the champions of the two sides, Lord Chancellor Ellesmere of equity, and Chief Justice Coke of common law. Coke contended that Ellesmere was perpetrating an unwarranted interference with common law jurisdiction. Ellesmere retorted that his object was the very different one of preventing an individual litigant from soiling his conscience by standing on his legal rights, when the circumstances were such that the dictates of fair dealing demanded their abandonment. Disobedience to this, as to any other injunction, would be followed by personal attachment by the order of the Chancellor. Coke having expressed his intention of releasing by habeas corpus anyone so imprisoned, matters reached a deadlock, and James I stepped in. He referred the whole matter to a committee of counsel, whose chairman was Bacon, the Attorney-General. The committee decided the dispute in favour of the Chancery, and injunctions of this nature flourished to such an extent that they came to be known as 'common injunctions', and were familiar instruments of procedure until the Judicature Act 1873.

The change-over from clerical to lay Chancellors had been inaugurated by the appointment of Sir Thomas More to succeed Wolsey in 1530, but it was not until over a hundred years had elapsed that the practice of appointing clerical Chancellors altogether ceased. Ellesmere was succeeded by Bacon, who did much to modernize and improve the procedure of the Court of Chancery. He in turn was succeeded by Williams, Bishop of Lincoln, a man well versed in politics but ignorant of the law. But he proved to be the last clerical Chancellor, and since 1672 none but a learned lawyer has held the office. In that year the Great Seal was delivered to Lord Nottingham, who has been called the 'father of equity'. It would be more accurate to call him the father of *systematic* equity, for he and his successors set equity on a new course. It underwent a transformation. Equity Reports had begun to appear in the reign of Mary I, but they were regarded simply as records and not as precedents. Chancellors continued to act according to the merits of the individual case, viewed according to their conception of the promptings of conscience. But from 1672 onwards equity gradually became a system of precedents, whose rigidity resembled more and more that of the common law. The eighteenth century was a time of legislative stagnation, and judicial precedent, legal and equitable, was left largely to mould the law of the future. But law and equity differed in that, while no part of the gigantic chessboard of human relations was left unscoured by law, there were many localities into which equity never intruded. There was no equity in substantive criminal law, little in the law of torts. There was much more in the law of contracts, and in the law of property the tail may almost be said to have wagged the dog, for through its centre ran the powerful bone of the trust.

Let us examine the work of the Court of Chancery. First would rank the decision of a multitude of cases on trusts. In one case a plaintiff would be seeking to have a will interpreted so as to establish a trust in his favour, over property which the defendant claimed as bequeathed to him unconditionally by the same will. In another the beneficiary of a trust would be accusing his trustee of a breach of trust, and asking the court to compel him to make good the loss. In a third the creditors of a trader would be seeking to upset a trust of property previously made by him, on the ground that his motive in making it was to withdraw it by anticipation from their reach. A fourth would be a case of a charitable trust, for no defined beneficiaries, but for a purpose; a trustee, for instance, having duly devoted part of a legacy to the erection of a church, would come to the court to ask for directions as to the disposal of the surplus.

Many cases of tort and contract would come before the court. The only remedy known to common law was damages. But in some torts, and notably in the case of nuisance, this was inadequate; the action of common law would resemble that of bolting the stable door after the escape of the horse, or, changing the metaphor, allowing Ahab to flout the rights of Naboth at the price of contemptuously flinging him a cheque for which he had not asked. Equity would, if satisfied that damages would be an inadequate remedy, issue an injunction, forbidding the defendant to start or continue the course of conduct of which the plaintiff complained. Again, the power to order the specific restitution of a chattel, which the legislature gave to the common law action of detinue in 1854, had long been employed by equity in the case of chattels of especial beauty or rarity, for the loss of which no amount of money could compensate their owners. In cases of contract, equity had, as well as the injunction, three other remedies, the decree for specific performance, the cancellation, and the rectification of written documents. But it must always be remembered that these equitable remedies could not, as could damages, be claimed as of right by a plaintiff who could make out his case, but were discretionary. Thus, for instance, equity would not, for obvious reasons, compel a person to fulfil a promise of marriage or personal services, but would leave the disappointed bride or employer to recover damages at common law.

A province of the land law much marked with the impress of

equity was the mortgage. The action of equity, as Maitland put it, turned the mortgage deed into one long suppression of the truth and suggestion of falsehood. The normal mortgage deed, before the changes introduced by the legislation of 1925, recited that, in consideration of a money loan, a landowner transferred a piece of land to the lender, the latter covenanting to transfer it back again if principal and interest were duly paid at the end of six months. If, however, the money was not then paid, the borrower, though he would remain liable to pay it, lost his land for ever. As the land at law belonged to the mortgagee, he could of course enter on it, sell it, or do what he liked with it. But equity regarded it as against conscience for him to do any of those things, except under conditions of which it approved. For it superimposed upon the mortgage deed the *equity of redemption*, whose vitality would survive the termination of the contractual right to redeem. What equity gave only equity could take away; a mortgagee who wished to get rid of the equity of redemption could do so only by obtaining from the Court of Chancery an antidote invented by itself, the decree for foreclosure.

The common law courts tried their hand at the administration of the estates of deceased persons, but they failed because of the inadequacy of their machinery for taking accounts, and administrative work in general. From them might be obtained vigorous action at the suit of one creditor, but not watchful superintendence over the rights of all. The framework of the Court of Chancery was, however, sufficiently flexible to enable it to view the question of administration as a whole. From early times the court had concurrent jurisdiction in this matter with the ecclesiastical courts, and by the end of the seventeenth century it openly disregarded them. When, in the nineteenth century, ecclesiastical jurisdiction in this matter became obsolete, administration of assets became the exclusive business of the Court of Chancery.

The same advantage in administrative machinery gave to Chancery an almost undisputed sway in all matters involving accounts. Thus the winding-up of companies, dissolution of partnerships, and taking of partnership accounts fell into the lap of Chancery, unchallenged by any rival.

What court heard appeals from the Chancery? We have seen that it was established in 1675 by the case of *Shirley* v. *Fagg* that the

House of Lords had jurisdiction to hear such appeals. But it was not the least part of the complaint against the procedure of the court in the early nineteenth century, expressed in the mordant satire of Dickens in *Bleak House*, that there was no intermediate tribunal of appeal from the Chancellor except the Chancellor himself, and where a Chancellor was, as Lord Eldon at the beginning of the nineteenth century, cursed with a demon of procrastination, appeals must often have died of neglect. The roots of the trouble lay partly in the paucity of the judicial staff, and partly in the abuses rampant in the official staff. The progress of the nineteenth century witnessed a gradual improvement in both these directions. The first step consisted of the addition of two Vice-Chancellors; and then in 1851 were instituted the Lords Justices of Appeal in Chancery, who stood to the Chancery in the same relation as that borne by Exchequer Chamber to the three common law courts, a Court of Appeal intermediate between it and the House of Lords. Appeals in Chancery were always, as we have seen, conducted by the method of a rehearing of the case.

So the English legal system presented the unique phenomenon of two parallel sets of courts, performing widely different work, employing different procedure, and awarding different remedies. The Court of Chancery administered equity, the three courts of Common Pleas, King's Bench, and Exchequer administered common law. The functions were, it is true, not quite mutually exclusive, for the Court of Exchequer had until 1842, as we have seen, a certain equitable jurisdiction, and Chancery had also a certain common law jurisdiction, which must not be left unnoticed, consisting chiefly of matters in which the king was concerned, and actions brought by or against the officers of the court. The equity jurisdiction of the Exchequer demands a brief explanation. The *cursus scaccarii* presented analogies both to common law and to equity procedure. The suggestion that the Crown was interested as a creditor in the result of a case, on which the writ of quominus was based, made it possible also to file a bill in equity in that court, which thus became an equity tribunal for the decision of disputes between the Crown and its subjects, and between individual subjects. That very principle of the Chancery, that it acted by personal constraint of the defendant, which made it so powerful against a private individual, proved its heel of Achilles as against the Crown. Chancery would not 'make a fool of itself' by issuing an injunction it could not enforce. But to one aggrieved by any action of the Government the Court of Exchequer proved a very reliable helper. The duties of the Attorney-General, as guardian of the Crown's interests, which kept him studious to see that the Crown got its rights, bound him also to see that the Crown did right. This duty of his could be invoked by making him defendant to a suit for a *declaratory judgment*, that is to say, a pronouncement by the Court of Exchequer that some course of action contemplated by the Government was illegal. Chancery would use the same remedy, in appropriate cases, where parties were simply asking to have their rights defined. But the quality of tribunals was productive of much inconvenience, and denial of justice. It is easy now to say that the one and obvious cure stared our ancestors in the face long before they adopted it. Such a hasty estimate ignores the essential gradualness of all reform. In this case the initial steps were taken in the direction of a pooling of facilities. By the Common Law Procedure Act 1854 the common law courts were given a certain power of granting an injunction or specific performance, and by the Chancery Amendment Act 1858, usually known as Lord Cairns' Act, Chancery acquired the power of ordering the payment of damages, in addition to or in substitution for either of those two remedies. But these provisions were resting-places, not goals. In 1873 Mr. Gladstone's administration brought about a much more comprehensive measure of reform, in the Judicature Act 1873, which came into force in 1875. This Act abolished altogether the three common law courts, the Court of Chancery, the Courts of Probate, Divorce, and Admiralty, and replaced them by a new Supreme Court of Judicature. The exact provisions of this Act, and an estimate of its significance, must be discussed in the next chapter.

8 The courts at the present day

Whereas the judicial system in America has been created continuously, that of England has simply grown up gradually over the centuries. It is useless for a student to bring to the study of the English system the 'tidy mind', which is looked upon as the ideal quality of a modern civil servant. For the system has not been planned, it has developed 'from hand to mouth', with a certain spontaneity, to meet contemporary needs. It has been necessary more than once to emphasize that we must never think of it in terms of 'the separation of powers', for this doctrine, which permeates the written American constitution, has never formed part of the unwritten English constitution. We shall see in the next chapter that the one point of contact with the doctrine which it has established is in the theory of the independence of the judiciary; and this theory did not assert itself until the beginning of the eighteenth century, and is even now incomplete.

Nor is it possible to think of the system in terms of centralization and decentralization, for it has oscillated between these two extremes. Its history has been shaped not by a fundamental document but by the forces of action and reaction.

The basic division is into criminal and civil courts, but even between these there is some overlapping, though much less than before the passing of the Courts Act 1971.

Criminal Courts

One aspect of the English character which has often aroused the surprise of foreigners is the cheerfulness with which all sections of the community will do arduous public work without remuneration. Just as sediment collects at the bottom of a bottle of wine, so work is thickest at the foot of the judicial ladder, and at the foot stand 'the great unpaid', the justices of the peace (J.P.s), who try over 97 per cent of all criminal cases. Since the days of Edward I, these justices have filled a most important place, or, rather, many places of great importance, in the scheme of everyday life. They began not as justices but as conservators of the peace. Statutes of Edward III in 1327 and 1330 provided for the appointment of 'good and lawful men' in every county to keep the peace; they must commit to prison those arrested and brought before them, to await the visit of the king's itinerant justices. Statutes of 1344 and 1360 gave them the power to conduct the actual trial of prisoners, and in 1388 it was enacted that they were to hold sessions four times a year. These statutes spelled disaster to the luckless sheriff, for they sterilized the sheriff's tourn, which had already by Henry II been deprived of all jurisdiction over serious crime. Denuded even of the cognizance of petty offences, it perished from inanition, and the triumphant justices took over its entire work.

But the justices came to fulfil many other than judicial functions. Much administrative work was given to them. The reign of Edward III provided a melancholy illustration of the ghastly truth that in the wake of war stalks plague. The Black Death more than decimated the population. Faced with a grave labour shortage, and the inevitable rocketing of wages which such a situation involves, king and Council, by the Ordinance of Labourers 1349, established a system of industrial conscription and gave to the justices the vital task of fixing wage-rates. This legislation set in motion a process, which gathered momentum as the centuries rolled by, of increasing the administrative work of the justices to such an extent that they became, in effect, the real rulers of the county. The great Elizabethan writer, Lambard, refers in his treatise *Eirenarcha* to the 'stacks of statutes' which heaped ever more duties on them. Their due performance of these duties could, as we have seen, be enforced by writ of mandamus issued by King's Bench. In 1888 the great Local Government Act transferred the bulk of their administrative duties to the newly created County Councils, but yet reserved to the justices part of their administrative character by retaining certain functions concerning, for example, drainage under the Public Health Acts, and their power to consent to the marriage of infants. They also retained their control over the County Police, who were henceforth to be administered by a standing joint committee of magistrates and members of the County Council. Since the Police Act 1964 many local police forces have been amalgamated, so that most forces cover areas comprising more than one county. For all the police forces outside London, where rather different arrangements exist, the police authorities consist as to two-thirds of members of constituent local councils, and as to one-third of local magistrates.

Many of the administrative functions of justices resembled wisdom teeth, in that they were the last to come and the first to go. The Act of 1888 left them with the judicial functions with which they started. In the medieval period the Star Chamber tended to exercise a large control over them, but the abolition of that court in 1641 had the effect of transferring supervision powers to the courts of common law.

It is an interesting point of comparison between the English and American conceptions of democracy that the latter has always appeared to demand election as the regular, and appointment as the very exceptional, method of filling public offices. Though Federal judges are appointed, State judges, in the vast majority of States, are elected. But in England any form of elected judiciary is unknown.[1] At one time parliamentary pressure to establish an elective magistracy was strong, but it is now some time since it subsided, and the principle that the Crown should appoint the justices came to be tacitly accepted as best suited to the genius of the English constitution. In practice, appointments are made by the Lord Chancellor, on the advice of the Lord Lieutenant of the county, who is himself guided by an Advisory Committee consisting for the most part of existing magistrates.[2]

The vast majority of justices are unlearned in the law and unpaid, though the Lord Chancellor in 1964 instituted a scheme for the compulsory training of new magistrates, which came fully into force in 1966, and is now regulated by the Administration of Justice Act 1973, and is quite extensive in content. Every now and then we find a retired judge or other eminent lawyer on a local bench, but the qualities which should carry most weight with

[1] Save for the solitary exception of the Recorder of London, who is elected by the Court of Aldermen of the City of London.

[2] These committees were first set up in counties in accordance with the recommendations of the Royal Commission on the Selection of Justices of the Peace in 1910, and now exist for the new local authority areas brought into being by the Local Government Act 1972.

Lords Lieutenant in making recommendations are character, experience, long residence in the neighbourhood, and a reputation for devotion to the interests of its inhabitants. When Lord Gardiner was Lord Chancellor (from 1964 to 1970) he stated several times that he was making efforts to enable more weekly wage-earners to be appointed to the bench, and this has been facilitated by allowing magistrates to claim financial loss allowances. At the same time the Justices of the Peace Act 1968 abolished *ex officio* J.P.s (such as mayors), except in the City of London, where the Lord Mayor and Aldermen remain as magistrates, but are supplemented by other J.P.s duly appointed as such. On points of law the justices are kept on an even keel by the advice of the Clerk to the Justices, who must, under the Justices of the Peace Act 1949, be a trained lawyer, and who, since 1970, has been empowered to deal with certain matters by himself. These include the issue of summonses, the adjournment of a hearing with the consent of the parties, and allowing further time for payment of sums enforceable by a magistrates' court.

A few justices are both trained and paid, for the Crown, on the advice of the Lord Chancellor, appoints metropolitan stipendiary magistrates for the metropolis of London, and, on request from any other local council, a stipendiary magistrate for that area. To be eligible for one of these posts a person must be a barrister or solicitor of seven years' standing. But, on the whole, the system of 'the great unpaid' may be said to have stood the test of time. On rare occasions an individual justice, through excitability or bias, will arouse public criticism, but such conduct is regarded as eccentric, and in no sense as characteristic.

Until recently magistrates sat in both Petty Sessions and Quarter Sessions, but the latter courts were abolished by the Courts Act 1971. Petty Sessions, now usually known simply as magistrates' courts, are very frequent. They have important pieces of civil jurisdiction, such as licensing of premises for the sale of alcohol, proceedings with regard to separation and maintenance orders and affiliation, small ejectment cases, and certain functions in connection with enforcement orders in the field of planning. Their criminal work, which is more bulky, consists mainly of the trial of the vast mass of non-indictable crimes, which Parliament continually swells by fresh additions. Under the Magistrates Courts Act

1952 they can also try certain indictable offences, and the list of such offences has been much increased by the Criminal Law Act 1977. This matter is too detailed for exhaustive description here; but, roughly speaking, the range of crimes which can be tried is considerably wider in the cases of 'children' (that is, those under fourteen) and 'young persons' (that is, those between fourteen and sixteen) than in the case of adults (i.e. those over sixteen). But adults and young persons cannot be tried summarily for indictable offences except with their consent, and this is not valid unless it has been explained to them that they have a right to demand trial by jury. The consent of the prosecution must also be obtained in cases concerning the property or affairs of the sovereign and certain other bodies, and that of the Director of Public Prosecutions when he is carrying on the prosecution. The result is that a man will usually elect for summary trial, unless either he is not guilty, or else, even though guilty, he feels he will have a better chance of acquittal before a jury. It should also be noted that the accused has the right to be tried by jury, if he so wishes, for any non-indictable offence for which he might be imprisoned for more than three months. Under the Children and Young Persons Acts 1933–69, a bench of magistrates, when dealing with a case in which a child or young person is being tried, without any adult co-defendant, is called a 'Juvenile Court', and must observe certain special rules, of which present space permits no details.[3] But in all cases of indictable crime, even of homicide, the initial stages are transacted before magistrates, who conduct the preliminary inquiry, and will dismiss the case where they consider that there is not sufficient evidence to go before a jury. Even where they do so, however, a bill of indictment may still be presented under the direction or with the consent of a High Court judge.

The Crown Court, already mentioned in Chapter 6, is a court of appeal from the decision of a magistrates' court, and also a court of original jurisdiction over all indictable crimes. Formerly Quarter Sessions had been the court in which many indictable crimes were tried. As far as any consistent principle can be discerned on which crimes were removed beyond the reach of Quarter Sessions, it

[3] See Walker and Walker, *The English Legal System*, 4th ed., Chapters 9 and 26.

appeared to be on account either of gravity, as in the cases of treason and murder, or of legal difficulties usually involved. Quarter Sessions took place at least four times a year. There was, of course, a jury, but the character of the judges differed according to whether the Quarter Sessions were held in a borough or a county. In a borough there was a single judge, known as the Recorder, who had to be a barrister of five years' standing, and who took time off from his normal practice at the Bar to act as a part-time judge. In the county the lay magistrates sat as judges, though with a chairman who, after 1938, had to possess legal qualifications. Now that Quarter Sessions have been swept away, the Crown Court is presided over by a professional judge, whether he be a High Court judge, Circuit Judge, or Recorder, who may sit with magistrates for some trials. Although High Court judges must be barristers, the Courts Act 1971 provides that either a barrister or a solicitor of ten years' standing may be appointed as a Recorder on a part-time basis; and the Administration of Justice Act 1973 extends the same rule to the appointment of any deputy Circuit Judge. A Circuit Judge must either have been a barrister of at least ten years' standing, or else have held the office of Recorder for at least three years. Thus the way to the Circuit Bench is now open to a solicitor after first serving for three years as a Recorder. Indeed a number of solicitors have now been appointed as Circuit Judges.

A magistrates' court can, at the instance of either prosecutor or defendant, *state a case*, that is to say, submit a question of law for determination by a Divisional Court[4] of the Queen's Bench Division of the High Court. The same power belongs to the Crown Court, but only in cases which have come to it from magistrates. A case may go up on 'case stated' even after it has been dismissed, which contrasts with the rule that the prosecution has no appeal from an acquittal by a jury.

It is convenient here to mention the Coroner's Court. The office of coroner is an old one. He was introduced originally as a royal official in the county to keep a check on the sheriff. But as the sheriff's powers were sapped by other agencies, so the coroner's duties became canalized. They are mainly concerned with the investigation of the causes of suspicious deaths. The function of the

---

[4] Two or three judges of the Division sitting together.

court is to accuse and not to try, but the Criminal Law Act 1977 has removed the former power of the Coroner's Court to find that a named person is guilty of murder, manslaughter or infanticide, a finding which was equivalent to an indictment. Today the justification for the court's continued existence is that it ensures that all deaths not readily explainable as caused by natural circumstances are adequately and publicly investigated.

In discussing the Court of King's Bench it was remarked that, though possessed of complete criminal jurisdiction, that court seldom used it, as in practice the vast majority of indictable crimes were tried at assizes or Quarter Sessions. The trial at bar by King's Bench was never satisfactory, for it gave an advantage, albeit largely illusory, to a rich man, not open to the purse of a poor man. By section II of the Administration of Justice (Miscellaneous Provisions) Act 1938, the criminal jurisdiction of the King's Bench Division of the High Court was reduced almost to vanishing point, and it was finally abolished by the Courts Act 1971.

Against an acquittal by a jury, the Crown has no appeal. Some writers have urged that we should do well to introduce the South African system, under which an appeal can be brought to determine a point of law, while the person who has been acquitted remains unaffected. Against a conviction, the prisoner has a right to appeal which was established, as we have seen, in 1907. This lay to the Court of Criminal Appeal, until that court was replaced, under the Criminal Appeal Act 1966, by the new Criminal Division of the Court of Appeal, to which such an appeal will now go. This right is absolute on a question of law; on a question of fact, or mixed law and fact, it is subject to the permission of the trial judge or the Court of Appeal. But in practice it is not very difficult to find some legal technicality on which to ground an appeal. It would, however, amount to a travesty of justice if the court were bound to allow mere technicalities to upset a conviction. This consideration weighed strongly with the farmers of the 1907 Act, alongside two others, (*a*) that a miscarriage of justice, such as occurred in the case of Adolf Beck, twice convicted by juries owing to mistaken identity, should never be allowed to recur, (*b*) that time should not be spent, money should not be wasted, the court should not be congested, with frivolous appeals. The satisfaction of these three postulates called for some nicety of adjustment. The court can affirm a conviction, or *quash*, that is to say reverse, a conviction, or they can substitute one verdict for another, as for instance manslaughter for murder. They can also pass a substituted sentence, where they consider that conviction on one count was correct, but on another incorrect. But they can affirm a conviction in spite of some error in law at the trial, provided that they are satisfied that no miscarriage of justice[5] is caused by this course, or, in plainer language, that, had the error not been made, the jury would still have arrived at the same verdict. If the appeal is against the sentence, they can alter it, though not always necessarily in the prisoner's favour. Thus an accused person may have his conviction on one charge quashed, but the sentence upon another charge could be increased, though the 1966 Act provides that the Court of Appeal may not pass a sentence in relation to a part of an indictment of which the accused remains convicted which would be of greater severity than the total sentence originally passed on him at his trial. Only one judgment shall be delivered, unless the question is one of law which impels the Court to use the power given to it of directing that separate judgments be given. Under the 1907 Act the Court could only order a new trial in a rare case where the trial might be regarded as a nullity. But, under the Criminal Appeal Act 1964, a retrial may now be ordered on the ground of fresh evidence, if the Court also considers that such a retrial is required in the interests of justice.

The 1907 Act, as amended by the Administration of Justice Act 1960, contains the further important provision that *either Crown or prisoner* has a further appeal to the House of Lords, subject to the conditions already mentioned above at page 54, and the 1960 Act adds a similar structure of appeal from the Divisional Court direct to the House of Lords in summary cases.[6] Thus a conviction quashed by the Court of Appeal might be restored by the House of Lords. This precise eventuality happened in the case of *Ball* in 1911. In the case of *Smith*, in 1961, the prisoner was convicted of the murder of a police officer by driving his car, with the officer clinging to it, at an increasing speed and on an erratic course, so

---

[5] Under the 1907 Act the court had to be satisfied that no 'substantial' miscarriage of justice was caused, but the 1966 Act deleted the word 'substantial' from the proviso.

[6] These conditions are relaxed in cases involving habeas corpus proceedings.

that the officer fell off and was run over by another car. On appeal to the Court of Criminal Appeal the verdict was reduced to manslaughter on the ground that the trial judge had not explained to the jury that the presumption that everyone intends the natural consequence of his acts is rebuttable (in this case possibly by the prisoner's assertion that he was in fear of arrest for being in possession of stolen goods, and that he only intended to shake the officer off). But the House of Lords restored the verdict of murder.[7] It should be remembered that it is improbable that a man should suffer punishment for a crime he has not committed, and that even if he should so suffer there is still the safeguard of the Crown's executive power of pardon. The Home Secretary can, and does, quite independently of any judicial appeal, take all sorts of evidence that cannot be produced in court, or pursued in a judicial inquiry, and will readily advise the Queen to award a 'free pardon' if his researches reveal that a convicted man is really innocent.[8] He may also, if he pleases, under section 19 of the 1907 Act, refer the whole case to the Court of Appeal, who shall hear and determine it as if it were an appeal by the person convicted. However, it should, of course, be borne in mind that any action of the Home Secretary to redress by these means a wrong that has been done may well take time, sometimes amounting to several years.

The Criminal Appeal Act 1968 consolidates almost all the enactments concerning appeals to the Criminal Division of the Court of Appeal, and from there to the House of Lords, though appeals from the Divisional Court to the House of Lords are still governed by the Administration of Justice Act 1961.

Civil courts

England has never had, and is probably the poorer through never having had, an official like the French *juge de paix*, resident in the *commune*, empowered in the last resort to decide petty disputes, but

---

[7] By the Criminal Justice Act 1967, section 8, however, a court or jury shall not be bound in law to infer that a person intended or foresaw a result of his actions by reason only of its being a natural and probable consequence of those actions; but shall decide whether he actually did intend or foresee that result by reference to all the evidence, drawing such inferences from the evidence as appear proper in the circumstances. It seems now that juries are directed in these terms, and that the possibly harsh effects of the House of Lords ruling in *Smith* have been lessened.

[8] See Newsam, *The Home Office* (Allen & Unwin, 1954), p.115.

concerned primarily by wise counsel and conciliation to prevent litigation. Prior to the establishment in 1846 of the new County Courts, whose function is solely judicial and which have, consequently, no affinity with the old shire court of the sheriff, civil justice was highly centralized. Apart from the jurisdiction of the Franchise Courts, the only way in which a civil case could be tried elsewhere than in London was by having recourse to the power given by the Statute of Westminster II 1285 to judges at assizes to try such cases at *nisi prius*.[9] But the Act of 1846 avoided much travel and much expense. A County Court judge was appointed by the Lord Chancellor, and he had to be a barrister of seven years' standing. But now the same judges who sit in the Crown Court also sit in the County Courts. Indeed, under the Courts Act 1971, all then existing County Court judges were appointed as Circuit Judges, and the latter posts replaced the former.

The jurisdiction of the County Court is hardly limited at all by the difficulty of the case, though it is restricted by the amount of the sum in dispute. The financial limits of its jurisdiction have been progressively raised over the years, and, though the general jurisdiction of the court is now governed by the County Courts Act 1959, this statute has been amended from time to time. In particular the financial limit for claims in contract and tort was raised by the Administration of Justice Act 1969 to £750, and then in 1977 to £2000. A mass of other judicial work has been put upon these courts over the years, and it may suffice to give but one example. The Matrimonial Causes Act 1967 gave to County Courts the jurisdiction to hear and determine undefended matrimonial causes, e.g. divorce. Indeed every matrimonial cause must begin in a County Court, though it must be transferred to the High Court if it ceases to be undefended, and it may be so transferred if some special difficulty about the case becomes apparent.

The High Court is part of the Supreme Court of Judicature, which was established in 1873 to take the place of the old exclusive central courts of law and equity, and other courts of special jurisdiction, the other parts being the Court of Appeal and the Crown Court. Though we may now truly say that the long-term effect of the Judicature Act has been to fuse together the systems of law and

9 See p. 80.

equity, in form the changes it made were mainly in the field of adjective law, in substituting one court with total for several courts with partial jurisdiction. The changes it made in substantive law are collected in the first ten sub-sections of section 25. The eleventh and last sub-section contains the residual provision that in all other matters in which there existed a 'conflict or variance' between the rules of law and equity, the rules of equity should prevail. This provision looks very momentous, but as a matter of fact there are few cases in which any reference has been made to it in the courts, for the simple reason that cases of genuine conflict are of exiguous dimensions. No conflict is involved in the trust relation; the trustee is legal owner, with a real right which he can assert as against anyone tampering with the trust property, but he is bound to exercise his ownership on behalf of the beneficiary, who has, however, not a real but a personal right, which is good not only as against the trustee himself, but as against any other person handling the trust property, with the vital exception of the man who purchases it without notice of the trust. Nor is there any conflict in the position that for a breach of a contract equity will refuse specific performance, but law will award damages. The Act has simply inflicted one more defeat on that enemy, dangerous because of its very inertia, circuity of action, that is to say the multiplication of suits on the same matter. In *Webster* v. *Cecil* in 1861, A and B had been negotiating for the sale of some property, and in the course of haggling the price was hovering round £2,250. A decided to clinch the bargain at this figure. But in his letter he inadvertently quoted £1,250 instead. Having realized his mistake as soon as he had posted the letter he took immediate steps to correct it. B proposed to nail him to the literal terms of his offer, and sued in equity for specific performance. Lord Romilly refused to accede to so unconscientious a claim, and left him to ask a court of common law, were he so disposed, for damages. Whether such an action was actually brought we do not know, but what would happen nowadays is that B would sue, not in the Court of Chancery, which no longer exists, but in the Chancery Division of the High Court, and the judge, who can award any remedy, whether legal or equitable, would refuse specific performance, and direct an inquiry as to damages, unless he should regard the contract as void at law. The Act has of course killed the common injunction, but this weapon is still active in the hands of the High Court, to restrain a litigant whose hands are tainted with fraud from suing in a foreign court.

The High Court was at first in five Divisions, but from 1880 onwards there have been three Divisions,[10] the Queen's Bench Division, Chancery Division, and for many years the Probate, Divorce, and Admiralty Division. This latter Division, however, was abolished by the Administration of Justice Act 1970, and replaced by the present Family Division. The 1873 Act, as amended, in the main allocates to the Chancery Division the work of the old Court of Chancery,[11] to the Family Division the work concerning marriage, children, and family property, and to the Queen's Bench Division the work of the former three common law courts,[12] together with Admiralty and price matters, which will be explained presently. To the judges is delegated the power of making certain changes in the allocation that they think proper,[13] and all High Court judges can sit in any Division, and can administer both law and equity. But in practice the specialization of the legal profession has pursued the course of 'old man river'. It has 'kept rolling along'. Lincoln's Inn is still a home of Chancery barristers. A young man going to the Bar must still make up his mind whether he intends to go for equity or for common law, and will tend to seek the advice of those who know whether he has the qualities suited to the one or to the other. At common law he will go on circuit, and be much concerned especially with criminal cases and in civil actions arising, as Lord Hewart once put it, out of 'collisions between two stationary motor-cars'; he will often have to address a jury and examine and cross-examine witnesses. His prospects, if he decides on equity, are very different. He will have nothing to do with crime at all; he will never address a jury, he will rarely examine, and still more rarely cross-examine, a witness. He

[10] The judges resolved in 1880 to amalgamate the original Common Pleas Division and Exchequer Division with the Queen's Bench Division.

[11] The title of Vice-Chancellor was revived by the Administration of Justice Act 1970, and is now used for the senior judge of the Chancery Division.

[12] With the curious exception that the equitable jurisdiction of Exchequer, which was in 1842 transferred to Chancery, is now exercised by the Queen's Bench Division.

[13] As occurred by the judges' resolution of 1880, which amalgamated three Divisions of the High Court to form the present Queen's Bench Division: see above, n.l.

will be largely concerned with cases, which hardly come within the designation of genuine litigation at all, where two relatives come to the court to find out their rights under a will, or a scheme is propounded for the expenditure of a charitable bequest. For the judges to use their powers to alter the allocation of functions would be a profitless and wanton proceeding.

The former Probate, Divorce, and Admiralty Division had jurisdiction over a somewhat heterogeneous group of matters. The diverse subjects of 'wills, wives, and wrecks' were herded into a juxtaposition that was hardly sympathetic, due entirely to the fact that all three topics formerly fell within the cognizance of courts of special jurisdiction, and that it was desirable to keep the number of Divisions as low as possible.

We have seen that Chancery wrested from the Ecclesiastical Courts most of the province of administration of the estates of deceased persons. Those courts retained only the formal business of granting probate of wills and letters of administration. Even this formal business was transferred in 1857 to a new Court of Probate. Today contentious probate cases are dealt with in the Chancery Division, while non-contentious probate matters fall into the Family Division. Under the Patents Act 1977 a special Patents Court was set up as part of the Chancery Division, just as there is a Commercial Court, and since 1970 an Admiralty Court, within the Queen's Bench Division. The Patents Court includes specialist non-lawyer judges, and it hears appeals concerning patents.

Prior to the Matrimonial Causes Act 1857 divorce was impossible in England except by the laborious process of a decree of separation *a mensa et thoro*[14] by the Ecclesiastical Courts, followed by a Private Act of Parliament. The Act of 1857 created the Divorce Court, to which was given jurisdiction not only in divorce, but also in nullity, judicial separation, and decrees for restitution of conjugal rights. With the great increase in divorce during the twentieth century (due not so much to a worsening of family relations, as to law reform which has facilitated the granting of divorces), this subject is today a major part of the jurisdiction of the new Family Division. It will not be forgotten, however, that undefended matrimonial causes are dealt with in the County Court.

[14] 'From board and health'.

The Court of Admiralty is of far greater antiquity. It had in medieval times criminal jurisdiction in cases of crimes committed on the high seas by British subjects, by the crews of British ships whether subjects or not, and in cases of piracy by perpetrators of any nationality. But this jurisdiction was transferred in 1536 to the judges of the common law courts, sitting under special commissions. In 1834 it was lodged permanently in the Central Criminal Court. The Admiralty's civil jurisdiction comprised both maritime and commercial law. Both came to England from abroad, the former from the Laws of Oleron, a collection of decisions given by the maritime court of that island, the latter, usually known as the Law Merchant, from the customs of the Italian merchants. Both, therefore, were of a strongly international character. In neither field was the jurisdiction of Admiralty exclusive. Much maritime law was administered in local courts of seaport towns, which endured until the Municipal Corporations Act of 1835. One court escaped the axe wielded by this Act, the Court of the Warden of the Cinque Ports. The domestic Law Merchant was administered in Courts of Piepowder,[15] matters involving transactions between British and foreign traders in the Courts of the Staple, set up in certain towns under the Statute of the Staple 1353. Besides the rivalry of these various courts, the Admiralty had to face the jealousy of the common law courts, when resented the activities of a court proceeding according to the Civil Law, and not the common law. The Long Parliament, which championed the cause of the common law against all rivals, took away almost all jurisdiction from the Admiralty. Modern legislation restored to it much of its civil jurisdiction, but its character, as Holdsworth points out, was changed. The law now enunciated by it had lost its international character, and had become common law,[16] and it did not again administer the Law Merchant. When the Courts of Piepowder and Courts of the Staple ceased to exist, the Law Merchant was taken over by the common law, by a process started by encroachment in the thirteenth and fourteenth centuries substantially aided by the efforts of Chief Justices Coke and Holt at the beginning and

---

[15] They owe this name to the idea that a business man is always in a hurry; he comes to the court 'with dusty feet', therefore an expeditious procedure is necessary.

[16] Though some of its rules, and notably in the important field of contributory negligence, have differed from those of the common law.

end respectively of the seventeenth century, and completed by the decisions of that great common law judge Lord Mansfield, in the latter part of the eighteenth century. So entirely did this process succeed in incorporating the law Merchant into the common law that Chief Justice Cockburn was able to say in 1875, 'The Law Merchant is neither more nor less than the usages of merchants and traders in the different departments of trade ratified by the decisions of Courts of Law.' In 1895 the judges used the powers of adjustment confided to them by the Judicature Act to establish a court within the Queen's Bench Division, commonly known as the Commercial Court, where a judge with special learning and experience in commercial matters may determine commercial cases with the expedition and technical skill which they generally demand. This Commercial Court was further reorganized by the Administration of Justice Act 1970. Criminal jurisdiction was never restored to the Admiralty. The civil jurisdiction which it received back under the facade of common law was known as the 'instance' jurisdiction. It consisted mainly of collisions at sea, and mortgages and other contracts concerning ships. But there was another very important part of its jurisdiction which the court retained throughout, and which, consequently, never lost its international character. This was the 'prize' jurisdiction, to decide the validity, according to international law, of the capture in time of war of an enemy or neutral ship. The Admiralty jurisdiction of the High Court was transferred to the Queen's Bench Division by the 1970 Act, and today there are two apparently separate courts, the Commercial Court and the Admiralty Court, which are in fact only special sittings of the Queen's Bench Division.

Mention of the Commercial Court should remind us of another court with a limited, though most important, commercial jurisdiction. This is the Restrictive Trade Practices Court, set up by an Act of 1956, which does not form a part of the High Court. The maximum number of its judges is fifteen; five must be judges in the usual sense of the term, three from the High Court, one from the Court of Session in Scotland, one from the Supreme Court of Northern Ireland; the rest (not more than ten) are laymen, appointed on the recommendation of the Lord Chancellor by reason of their knowledge of or experience in industry, commerce, or public affairs. The objects of the institution of the court, whose original powers were amended by the Resale Prices Act 1964, are (*a*) the registration and judicial investigation of certain restrictive trading agreements; (*b*) the prohibition of such agreements when found to be against the public interest; (*c*) to prohibit the *collective*, but provide for the *individual*, enforcement of conditions regulating the resale price of goods if, but only if, they are shown to be in the public interest.

The Courts Act 1971, while mainly concerned with replacing the former courts for the trial of crimes on indictment by the new Crown Courts, makes one further important change to the character of the High Court. Since its creation in 1873 the High Court had sat only in London in the Law Courts built in Victorian times in The Strand, although some civil cases which would otherwise have been heard before the Queen's Bench Division in London were tried locally at assizes. The 1971 Act, however, provided that the High Court should have jurisdiction to deal with civil cases throughout England and Wales, and there is now no statutory limitation on where it may sit. This new peripatetic character of the High Court applies to all its Divisions; and the flexibility of the system is increased by permitting High Court judges to release some civil cases from their lists for trial before Circuit Judges. The Act also puts the administration of all County Courts, the Crown Court, and the High Court under the direction of the Lord Chancellor, so that all in all it is probable that the Courts Act 1971 is the most major reform of the English court system since the Judicature Act 1873. It simplifies the court structure, deploys 'judge-power' as flexibly as possible, secures the efficient administration of all court services, and makes both criminal and civil courts available to most people within a reasonable travelling time from their homes.

Apart from the decision of 'cases stated' by the justices of the peace, and review of their proceedings on order for certiorari,[17] the High Court has, in its collective form,[18] no criminal jurisdiction. The Court of Appeal had, until the Criminal Appeal Act 1966, absolutely none. Its civil jurisdiction is entirely appellate. Prior to

---

[17] These functions are discharged by a Divisional Court, i.e. of two or more judges of the Queen's Bench Division sitting together.

[18] As to the criminal jurisdiction of the Queen's Bench Division, see pp. 64, 79, 113.

1934 it heard appeals only from the High Court, which in turn heard appeals from the County Court. As appeals from the Court of Appeal to the House of Lords were unrestricted, a case might have to go through four tribunals, a state of affairs productive both of delay and of needless expense. So the Administration of Justice (Appeals) Act 1934 provided that appeals from the County Court should go direct to the Court of Appeal, and that appeals should go from the Court of Appeal to the House of Lords only by permission of one of those courts. So it is true to say that nowadays comparatively few cases run through more than two tribunals. There is also now even provision, by the Administration of Justice Act 1969, for a civil appeal to go direct from the High Court[19] to the House of Lords, 'leap-frogging' the Court of Appeal, where a point of law of general public importance is involved, and the point of law *either* relates wholly or mainly to the construction of an enactment or statutory regulation, which has been fully argued in the proceedings and fully dealt with in the judgment, *or* is one in respect of which the High Court was bound by a decision of the Court of Appeal or of the House of Lords in previous proceedings, and was fully considered in the judgments given by the Court of Appeal or the House of Lords in those previous proceedings. The Court of Appeal can affirm or reverse a decision of the High Court or County Court, or send it back for a new trial, if the judge has put the wrong questions to the jury.

The House of Lords is the final court of appeal in civil matters from all courts in England, Wales,[20] Scotland, and Northern Ireland, and hears about fifty appeals a year.[21] It has already been pointed out that the House has dual functions, legislative and judicial. In the exercise of either it is still the same body, but a very

[19] Including the Divisional Court.

[20] There are no courts peculiar to Wales. It is interesting, however, to notice that in modern times some sensible concessions have been made to Welsh patriotism. The Welsh Courts Act 1942, which repeals an Act of 1536, authorizes the use of the Welsh language in any court sitting in Wales; and the Lord Chancellor is empowered, with the assent of the Treasury, to make regulations as to the provision of interpreters. The Welsh Language Act 1967 also allows Welsh to be spoken by any party, witness, or other person in the course of legal proceedings in Wales, and gives authority for official documents to be published in Welsh.

[21] As pointed out above, the House of Lords is also the ultimate court of appeal for criminal cases in England, Wales, and Northern Ireland. But its criminal jurisdiction has never been extended to Scottish cases.

strong usage has, as we have seen, established itself that when the House is sitting as a final appellate court, no peers unlearned in the law attend. The actual composition of the body who in fact exercise the judicial functions of the House has already been described,[22] and here it need only be added that as Scottish appeals come to the House, and as Scots Law in many respects differs from English Law, it is important that at least two of the Lords of Appeal should have practised at the Scottish Bar, or at any rate should have a thorough knowledge of the Scottish system.

Appeals from the instance jurisdiction of the Admiralty Court in the Queen's Bench Division go, as do appeals from the other two Divisions, to the Court of Appeal. But appeals from the prize jurisdiction go to the Judicial Committee of the Privy Council. The history and character of this court has already been discussed and its functions enumerated.[23]

Although for most purposes the structure of courts within England and Wales, and indeed within the whole United Kingdom, is self-sufficient, there is one modification introduced by the European Communities Act 1972, which brought into effect the United Kingdom's membership of the European Economic Community. Where any question regarding the interpretation or validity of the Treaties establishing the European Community, or of the acts of the institutions of the Community, is raised before any court or tribunal of any member state, including the United Kingdom, that court or tribunal may request the European Court of Justice to give a ruling thereon before proceeding further with the case in hand. Furthermore such a reference to the European Court *must* be made if there is no further judicial remedy against the ultimate decision of the court or tribunal concerned. Thus if such a question arises in the House of Lords it must be referred for a ruling by the European Court before the ultimate decision is given in the case by the Lords. To this extent, therefore, the House of Lords may be said to be no longer always the ultimate court of appeal in the United Kingdom. But the provision in the 1972 Act will be likely to affect only a very limited number of cases, and it must be borne in mind that the final decision in a case, even where the European Court has made a

22 See p. 55.
23 See p. 59.

ruling (which will be incorporated in the eventual decision in the case), rests with the House of Lords.

9 The place of judges in the Constitution

By devious routes we have now returned to our starting-point, and in our journey have left unanswered some questions of fundamental importance. Judges are the guardians of the gate of ordered society; to them belongs the sacred office of ensuring that the principles of right dealing according to law are pursued by private citizens towards each other, and towards the State, and, most crucial of all, by the State towards private citizens. They must administer justice 'without fear or favour, affection or ill-will'. The first question is, by what means are judges sheltered from executive compulsion or influence, and shepherded into that haven of serene detachment which is alone conducive to the formation of dispassionate judgments on the troubled affairs of mankind? To answer this, we must determine what is meant by judicial independence, and see how far it is secured in the English system. As comparison with other systems is the aptest of methods for the true understanding of one's own, we must in this inquiry cause our minds, Puck-like, to 'put a girdle round the earth', resting momentarily with pointing finger on this system and on that. But when this question has been solved, another, more difficult in being more generalized, will demand investigation. What is it that, in the estimate of all competent foreign observers, causes the British judicial system to enjoy a dignity and prestige certainly equal to, and usually greater than, that of any other Bench in the world?

The theory of judicial independence

Without the realization of the ideal of judicial independence, equality of all citizens before the law, and the mutual confidence which is begotten of the consciousness of that equality, would be impossible. This is recognized in every civilized country. Thus article 112 of the Soviet Socialist Constitution reads: 'Judges are independent and subject only to the law.' Article 64 of the Constitution of the Republic of Poland lays down in para. 3 that 'The judges are independent in the discharge of their judicial duties', and in para. 4 that 'the sentences of the courts may not be changed or annuled by other organs or authorities'. Thus is the ideal envisaged and expressed; by what steps can it, according to English conceptions, be attained?

1. Judges must be kept clear of political bias. This is ensured as far as possible by their exclusion, under the Act of Settlement 1701, from the House of Commons. This exclusion is extended to Circuit Judges, but not to Recorders, other than the Recorder of London, or to lay magistrates. But the safeguard is necessarily incomplete, for no statutory provision could control the play of ideas, and even if a man be strong enough to banish from his mind the political predilections of former days, he will preserve them, whether as cherished guests or as parasites, in his heart. And a judge who happens to be a peer is not excluded from the House of Lords; some, indeed, are necessary and weighty members of the House. But it can be said with some confidence that the little finger of etiquette is thicker than the loins of statutory prohibition, and a Lord of Appeal in Ordinary who should voice opinions in the House or outside it which revealed him as a partisan of one of the political parties would be guilty of a public solecism of the gravest dimensions, from which his reputation would hardly recover.

2. A judge must be kept free from political pressure. That is to say, the beginning, continuance, and end of his judicial life must be so shaped that he is enabled to regard with indifference alike the smiles and the frowns of the highest Ministers of the Crown. The appointment to a judicial post must be made in the hands of someone who can be relied upon to base his choice on those qualities, and on those qualities alone, which make for judicial fitness; and no whit less vital is it that, once appointed, a judge should have a guaranteed security of tenure. In England the Queen appoints most superior judges on the advice of the Lord Chancellor, and indeed magistrates are even directly appointed by the Lord Chancellor. The position of this great Minister is perhaps the most baffling of many paradoxes to which the genius of the English governmental system has been brought by its peculiar and meandering progress down the stream of development. The doctrine of judicial independence represents, in effect, its sole accep-

tance of the principle of the separation of powers. But the whole status of the Lord Chancellor, the head of the judicial hierarchy, cuts the ground from under the feet of that very doctrine. He was in medieval times the greatest of all Ministers of the Crown; he is, though overshadowed by the Prime Minister, in official precedence the greatest Minister still. Therefore, with the elaboration of the modern system of party government, he became an indispensable member of party Cabinets, with whose access of power he himself comes into office, and with whose demise he goes out of office. For he whose judicial appointees must enjoy security of tenure has none himself. More, as Speaker of the House of Lords he does not, like the Speaker of the House of Commons, pretend to impartiality, but is one of the government's most vocal spokesmen. How, then, seeing that he is bound by the doctrine of Cabinet solidarity to utter no discordant note to mar the harmonious chorus which, whatever the private bickerings of its members, must invariably assail the public ear, can it be pretended that, when a seat on the Bench falls vacant, he can resist the temptation to make a 'political appointment' of some 'good party man' favoured by his non-legal colleagues, who view a judgeship primarily as a reward for good political service? The answer is that he is prevented, not by anything in the visible nature of the office, but by much of its traditions. These will be so potent as to galvanize the weakest of Chancellors into resisting all suggestions, blandishments, and demands by his colleagues; the serried ranks of his illustrious predecessors speak to him with one voice, and tell him that judicial appointments are his and his alone.[1] In a word, the force of tradition will insulate his judicial appointments from his other executive functions. It cannot indeed be said that political appointments have never been made. The case put by Thackeray of the dancing barrister—'but he was related to a Duke, and it was expected that the Lord Chancellor would give him something very good'—may pass as a cynical irreverence; but political

---

[1] The appointment of the Lord Chief Justice, and of a small number of other superior judges, differs from other judicial appointments, being in the hands of the Prime Minister. But even in the case of these appointments, successive Prime Ministers since the Second World War have followed the practice of taking the advice of the Lord Chancellor and of senior members of the Bar, and thus selecting most appointees without political bias.

appointments dwelling within the realm of fact may take one of two forms, that of a reward to a lawyer-politician who has grown grey in the service of the party, and that of an inducement to the occupant of a 'safe' seat in the House of Commons to quit it in favour of a Minister who has lost his seat at an election. The former type of appointment is very rare, the latter perhaps a little more common. But in making either, a Chancellor must be troubled with misgivings, which have been in general abundantly justified by the events; for such appointments have rarely been crowned with success.

But it would be of little use merely to ensure that judicial appointments are exclusively in the hands of a great lawyer,[2] who is in a position to know the most suitable men among the leaders of the Bar, if the chosen judge were liable to be ousted from his post should his decisions fail to please the party in power, or if the executive were free to hamper him in the discharge of his duties. Medieval judges were by no means independent in the modern sense. They were regarded as servants of the Crown, to be dismissed at the king's pleasure; and bearing this fact in mind we may be induced on the one hand to moderate our indignation at the majority of judges who decided against Hampden in the case of *Ship Money*, or at Scroggs who could say *ex cathedra* that 'it is never lawful to say anything against government', and on the other to redouble our veneration for Gascoigne who fearlessly committed Prince Hal for contempt, and Coke who laid down that the king cannot alter the law, or create a new offence, but can only admonish his subjects to observe the existing laws.

In 1701 the Act of Settlement removed the judges beyond the reach of the executive arm, by rendering them irremovable except by a process which is equivalent to an exercise of legislative power. Indeed, they receive under it better protection than they would have received had it been laid down simply that in order to remove one of them a statute is required. For the House of Lords cannot be by-passed on this issue, as it can under the Parliament Acts 1911 and 1949, because the Act of 1701, as re-enacted in 1925, requires that an address for removal be presented to the king by *both*

---

[2] The Lord Chancellor also has special responsibilities in connexion with the initiation of law reform: see, e.g., the Law Commissions Act 1965.

Houses. Thus a judge can be sure that he cannot be swept off the Bench on the wave of the ephemeral and emotional feeling of a political majority, but only by an opinion of his personal or professional unworthiness endorsed by the chief men of his own profession, for the House of Lords in its debate would naturally attach great, even decisive, importance to the views expressed by the Lords of Appeal in Ordinary. The provision has never yet been invoked in relation to an English judge, though an Irish judge, Sir Jonah Barrington, was removed from office by this process in 1830. It does not apply to Circuit Judges and justices of the peace, who can be removed by the Lord Chancellor, nor does it apply to colonial judges, who can be appointed for a term, and removed by the Foreign and Commonwealth Secretary. But provision for a retirement age for inferior judges has been extended to superior judges by the Judicial Pensions Act 1959; and the Administration of Justice Act 1973 authorizes the Lord Chancellor to declare vacant the office of any superior judge who is incapacitated from resigning, for example, as the result of a stroke or mental illness.

But what is to prevent the executive using its majority in the Commons to force a judge's resignation by the indirect method of cutting down his salary to a nominal sum, for the House of Lords cannot, under the Parliament Act 1911, reject or amend a Bill certified by the Speaker as a Money Bill? Well, of course, no rampart is safe against the onslaught of the sovereign legislature, but the salaries of judges are safeguarded as far as is possible by being charged on the Consolidated Fund; that is to say, they do not, like Supply Services, have to be annually voted, and most recent provision for *increasing* these salaries, and for regulating judges' pensions, is contained in the Judges' Remuneration Act 1965 and the Administration of Justice Act 1973, under which salary increases may be made by governmental regulation. When, in 1931, the National Economy Act empowered the Treasury to reduce the salaries of 'servants of the Crown', and the Treasury proposed to include the judges under this designation, the judges felt bound to protest. They did so not on any selfish financial grounds, but simply because the proposal ignored, and threatened to reverse, the emancipation from executive control which had been given to them by the Act of Settlement.

3. A judge must be free to speak boldly in his judicial capacity.

Justice could never be done were a judge to be compelled by fear of the law of defamation, always inclined to be over-favourable to plaintiffs, to pick and choose all his utterances on the Bench. So a judge enjoys absolute privilege, that is to say he cannot be sued for any such utterance.[3] It is safe to say that only on very rare occasions has a tactless or over-zealous judge abused this privilege; and a superior judge would anyway be aware that a grave abuse might lead to an address for his removal under the Act of Settlement procedure. No more significant index could be provided of the state of public confidence in judicial integrity than the virtual absence of resort to this process through a period now approaching three centuries.

4. English judges have for three centuries been unanimous in the view that they should be called upon to give decisions only as between litigants of flesh and blood, and not on hypothetical cases put to them by the executive or anyone else. American public opinion has gone even further, in condemning all collusive litigation, a device to which resort is sometimes had for the purpose of establishing a doubtful point of law. But litigation, whether genuine or collusive, there must be. English judges draw a clear line between the atmosphere of the forum and that of the debating-hall, considering that the latter is not conducive to the establishment of precedents that will advance the general cause of justice. Lord Hewart has immortalized for us the debate in which the Law Lords fought and won a grim fight against a proposed clause in the Rating and Valuation Bill 1925, which would compel the judges to give rulings on points of law submitted by the Minister of Health. It is fair to remark, however, that in Canada the Governor-General in Council has power to demand the opinion of the Supreme Court on any question of law,[4] and Canadian opinion has not found this power to be incompatible with the theory of judicial independence. Indeed the recent proposals for a new Constitution for Canada, included in the Constitutional Amendment Bill 1978, retain this power.

The four safeguards just discussed guarantee the complete free-

---

[3] Nor, as was decided in *Sirros* v. *Moore* in 1974, for assault or false imprisonment resulting, it was alleged, from his decisions.

[4] See Kennedy, *Constitution of Canada*, p. 395.

dom of judges to administer justice according to law. But more is needed to ensure public confidence in their impartiality; and the law has established several rules which should allay any doubts on this score:

1. It cannot be too widely known that it has been established by decided cases that a judge cannot try any case in which he is personally interested.

2. A judge must, in a contested case, give reasons for his decision.

3. Most important of all, publicity is of the essence of all judicial administration. The public have a right to be admitted to any court, limited only by the capacity of the building. Of course a judge can clear his court if spectators behave improperly therein, and there are certain proceedings which must, under special statutory provisions, be heard *in camera*, such as those which come under the Official Secrets Acts 1911 and 1920. Judges in domestic proceedings have a discretion to exclude the public in cases where evidence of an indecent character is to be submitted, and medical evidence in nullity cases is usually taken *in camera*. The reports of committal proceedings before examining magistrates[5] are restricted by the Criminal Justice Act 1967, and the publication of names or pictures of victims of rape, or of defendants charged with rape, is now prohibited by the Sexual Offences (Amendment) Act 1976. But the broad rule is that all judicial administration must be open to popular inspection, a rule which was neatly expressed by Lord Hewart in the aphorism, 'Justice must not only be done; it must be manifestly seen to be done.'

This feature of enforced publicity has now been followed by the numerous and variegated administrative tribunals, whose multiplication tends so greatly to complicate the study of the English governmental system. Into the difficult territory of administrative law, in which this thorny subject lies embedded, we can, in a survey such as the present, take only the most fleeting glance. To its inevitable complexities additional obstacles have been added by the absence of any uniformity as to nomenclature. American writers tend to treat administrative law as covering the same ground as that covered by constitutional law. When the French

[5] See p. 111.

talk of *droit administratif* they refer to the hierarchy of courts, parallel to the ordinary courts of law, which try disputes between private citizens and government officials. This institution aroused the suspicions of Dicey, who would allow no merit to any system which withdraws the acts of the official from the cognizance of the ordinary courts of law. Dicey was undiscerning in his praise for the English at the expense of the French system, for it was based on the assumption that the administrative courts tend to favour the official, a view which is by no means borne out by the facts. Indeed, the facts point to the opposite conclusion to that reached by Dicey, in that in France a private citizen who can make out a case against the State is certain of substantial redress, whereas in England he was, until 1948, thrown on the resources of the petition of right, which moved in shackles forged by the medieval common law. The anomalous position, prior to the Crown Proceedings Act, 1947, was that a subject could, by petition of right, recover property, or damages for a breach of contract, other than a contract of service, or one whereby the Crown purported to fetter its future executive action, but not for a tort. It was urged by one witness before the Committee on Ministers' Powers in 1932 that the French system of administrative courts might with advantage be introduced in England, but the Committee were unanimous in rejecting the suggestion, on the ground that the French system was arrived at owing to the peculiar course taken by certain aspects of French history; that, like Canary wine, it 'would not travel'; and that the true remedy for the unsatisfactory position of the subject as litigant against the Crown lay not in adopting a foreign system but in modernizing our own. This much-needed reform was effected by the Act of 1947, which abolished the petition of right, and provided that a Government Department may be sued by an ordinary action in any case in which it would have lain, and also, subject to certain exceptions, in cases of tort.

The mention of the Committee of 1932 brings us to the most vivid, universal sense in which the term 'administrative law' is used in England. Montesquieu erred in assuming that the English Constitution has developed along the lines of the doctrine of the separation of powers. Even Alexander Hamilton, who believed in it so fervently that he instilled its spirit into every phrase of the American Constitution, admitted that it could not be applied with entire consistency, and the course of American history has brought into being many bodies, such as the Interstate Commerce Commission, which perform all three functions of government. The truth is that while the legislative and judicial functions, though overworked, may sometimes rest, the executive must needs work twenty-four hours out of the twenty-four, for throughout parliamentary recesses and judicial vacations *things must still be done*, and experience has shown that things cannot adequately be done by those most qualified to do them unless they are allowed both to make rules and to decide disputes, to encroach, that is to say, to a considerable extent both on the legislative and on the judicial sphere. This is what the legislative is to an ever-increasing extent empowering the executive to do. This situation makes it necessary to examine briefly two salient topics:

(a) *The function of the courts with regard to the exercise of delegated legislative powers*

While the major part of the work of the Supreme Court of the United States consists in testing the validity of Acts of Congress by the criterion of their harmony with the Constitution, the duty of the English courts in relation to statutes is simply to apply and interpret them. But the gulf separating the functions of English and American judges is being continually narrowed by the doctrine of *ultra vires*, which must grow in proportion to the increase of the volume of delegated legislation. Acts such as the Housing Acts are constitutions in miniature. Parliament lays down a comprehensive measure for general slum clearance, but has neither the time nor the machinery for supervising its local application. It leaves the details to be filled in partly by the local authority, partly by the Department of the Environment. Should a landlord object to a demolition order, the jurisdiction of the courts to hear him depends on the view they take of the meaning of the enabling words, that is to say, the words in the Act which allowed the order to be made. Should these be set in the form that the orders are to have the same effect as if contained in the Act, the view of the House of Lords, expressed in the *Lockwood Case*,[6] is that the courts have no power to rule them to be invalid. But on the other hand the

[6] See p. 3.

House of Lords has laid down, in *Minister of Health* v. *R.*, *ex parte Yaffe* in 1931, that if a provision in an order is in conflict with a provision in the enabling Act, it then rests with the courts to detect the inconsistency and declare that the order must give way to the Act, and so lack validity. A study of these enabling sections reveals several varieties, for Parliament has framed them without any sort of systematic plan. Sometimes a Minister has been given power even to alter the Act; this type of clause is known as 'the Henry VIII Clause', from the Statute of 1539, which enabled that king to legislate by proclamation; the Committee on Ministers' Powers considered its tendency to be dangerous, and that its employment should be limited to cases of extreme urgency. As a general guide it may be said that the courts will be very reluctant to hold that Parliament has intended to abandon its exclusive control over taxation by delegating the taxing power to a Minister or anyone else, and will so hold only under the stress of words which can be interpreted in no other way.[7] Again, as we have seen, complete absence of ambiguity would be required before the courts would decide that a Minister had been empowered to make an order restraining subjects from appealing to them for redress.

(b) The relation of the courts to quasi-judicial and administrative powers wielded by other bodies

Though the courts are the stalwart and reliable champions of the subject, both against his fellow-subjects and against the executive, they lack the equipment for the decision of many technical questions. Recognizing this fact, Parliament has created many tribunals which perform functions analogous, in greater or lesser degree, to those performed by the courts properly so called. These exhibit a bewildering variety of characteristics. Three examples must here suffice.

  (a) The Medical Act 1956 (formerly an Act of 1858) constitutes the General Medical Council the custodians of the honour of the

[7] The Abnormal Importations Act 1932 empowered the Board of Trade to add articles at discretion to a list of articles which should bear an especially high import duty; the Emergency Powers Act 1939 empowered the Treasury to impose charges in connexion with any scheme of control authorized by the Defence Regulations, subject to the safeguard that orders should lapse, unless approved within 28 days by a resolution of the House of Commons.

profession, with wide disciplinary powers over registered medical practitioners. Section 33 of the Act draws a distinction between causes for the removal of a name from the register. If the cause is conviction for crime, the discretion of the Council is unfettered, but if it is 'infamous conduct in any professional respect', the Council can act only 'after due inquiry', and an order for certiorari will be granted to quash the direction if the Court considers that such due inquiry has not been held. The House of Lords, in *R.* v. *General Medical Council, ex parte Spackman*, in 1943, interpreted the original limitation in the 1858 Act as rendering deficient an inquiry which had ignored a claim by a medical practitioner to adduce evidence which, for reasons of his own, he had not adduced before a divorce judge. The 1956 Act now provides that any finding of fact shown to have been made in matrimonial proceedings in courts of the United Kingdom or Ireland, shall be conclusive evidence of the fact found.

(*b*) Courts-Martial are established under the Army Act for the trial of offences against military law. The Civil Courts will by order for prohibition prevent a Court-Martial from trying anyone not subject to military law. A person convicted by a Court-Martial may appeal to the Courts-Martial Appeal Court, established under an Act of 1951, on obtaining the leave of that Court; and, under the Administration of Justice Act 1960, a further appeal lies to the House of Lords.[8]

(*c*) Under a series of Acts of Parliament, of which the most important is now the Social Security Act 1975, there is a structure of tribunals dealing with claims for various pensions, allowances, and benefits which are the centrepiece of the compulsory National Insurance scheme regulating the modern welfare state. Thus all claims for unemployment benefit, sickness benefit, child benefit, maternity allowance, industrial injury benefit, death grant, special hardship allowance, retirement pension, and a host of other related benefits, must first be adjudicated upon by a local insurance officer in the Department of Employment or the Department of Health and Social Security. Thereafter an appeal may be heard

---

[8] Subject to the same conditions applying to other criminal appeals to the Lords: see pp. 54, 114. The Courts-Martial (Appeals) Act 1968 now consolidates the provisions concerning all appeals in this field.

by an independent Local Appeal Tribunal, consisting of a lawyer chairman and two lay members, one drawn from a panel of employers, and the other from a panel of employees. A further and final appeal lies to the National Insurance Commissioner in London.[9]

Are the functions of these tribunals judicial, or do they fall into the category of quasi-judicial? The very use of this hybrid word shows how difficult is the work of classification. The conclusion to which the cases lead us is that a quasi-judicial body must act according to the principles of natural justice, but need not in every respect conform to the strict rules laid down for courts of law. Thus the rules of natural justice, namely that no man must adjudicate in a dispute in whose outcome he is himself interested, and that he must hear both sides, are common to both judicial and quasi-judicial bodies. But a quasi-judicial body can make its final decision in the absence of the parties. On the other hand, its members do not enjoy absolute privilege; that is to say, the privilege can be removed if a plaintiff can show that they were actuated by malice. The most typical example of a quasi-judicial body at the present day is that of an inquiry. Where a planning application has been made, or a proposal is put forward for a new road, objectors must normally be given the opportunity to appear or to be represented at a public local inquiry, which must in its proceedings accord with the rules of natural justice. But the eventual decision of the issues at stake is reached after the conclusion of the inquiry, usually by the responsible government Minister, and need not necessarily be in accordance with the weight of the evidence at the inquiry. The report of the actual inquiry will be only part, albeit an important part, of the information upon which the decision is ultimately based. A tribunal, on the other hand, must reach a decision in accordance with the relevant law and evidence, as adduced before it at the hearing, and is thus truly a judicial body, even though outside the ordinary court hierarchy.

The recommendations of the Committee on Ministers' Powers in 1932 were never fully endorsed by the legislature, but more generous treatment was accorded to the Franks Committee on

[9] The Small Claims Courts in London and Manchester, consisting of a lawyer acting as the sole arbitrator, and hearing claims in contract and tort up to a maximum of £350, are in essence special tribunals which hive off very minor cases from the County Court.

Administrative Tribunals and Enquiries, which reported in 1957. Not all tribunals are covered by the resulting Tribunals and Inquiries Act 1971 (re-enacting the original 1958 Act), nor are all of those which are covered bound by all its provisions, but in general the Act has effected four main reforms: (*a*) the establishment of a standing Council on Tribunals, to keep the operation of both tribunals and enquiries under review; (*b*) the chairmen of tribunals are selected by the 'appropriate authority' (normally the Minister concerned) from a panel of persons appointed by the Lord Chancellor; (*c*) parties to tribunal proceedings are given a right of appeal on points of law to the High Court, or can require the tribunal to state a case for its consideration; (*d*) tribunals and Ministers deciding issues after public inquiries have been held must give reasons for their decisions. Furthermore, decisions of the courts in recent years have clarified the strength of the English principles of judicial review of the exercise of powers by other authorities. In *Ridge* v. *Baldwin* in 1964, the House of Lords declared that the dismissal of a Chief Constable by his police authority without his having been given an adequate opportunity to answer the complaints against him was illegal and void; and the Lords went on to stress that it mattered not at all whether the power to dismiss a police officer was classified as judicial or administrative. In *Anisminic Ltd.* v. *Foreign Compensation Commission* in 1969, the Lords went on to assert the courts' power of review even where an inferior authority was empowered by Parliament to make a decision which 'shall not be called in question in any court of law'. The result has been that Parliament's efforts to grant 'judge-proof' powers have been of no avail, and the traditional distinction between judicial, quasi-judicial, and even administrative powers and duties is of far less importance than formerly.

Some executive discretions do, however, exist. A good example is the power given by the British Nationality Act 1948 to the Home Secretary to confer the status of British subject and citizen of the United Kingdom and colonies on an alien. This naturalization can be withdrawn by the same authority without cause shown, and the alien has no remedy. The Home Secretary can use any means he chooses for arriving at his decision, and he is not bound by the rules of natural justice. In short, the whole matter belongs exclusively to the executive, and the judiciary has no sort of control. Yet even in this area of law there are some signs that executive power is on the wane, for recent statutes have introduced an element of review into the Home Secretary's previously unfettered powers over deportation and immigration. In interpreting a statute as having conferred an executive discretion, the courts in effect perform an act of self-abnegation. Lord Camden in *Entick* v. *Carrington* in 1765 laid down the great principle that 'our law knows nothing of State necessity'; it is useless for any public official to attempt to excuse an illegal act as having been demanded by the interests of the community. But in war the legislature must needs endow the executive with comprehensive powers under the stress of which many of the most cherished rights of the subject fall into abeyance. It is not expedient that dangerous persons should roam at large; therefore one of the most necessary powers is that of ordering their detention. Both the Defence of the Realm Act 1914 and the Emergency Powers Act 1939[10] endowed the executive with the necessary authority in wartime to issue regulations for the better realization of this purpose. Dangerous persons are commonly litigious persons, and in the course of both wars the action of the executive was called in question before the House of Lords. In 1917, in *R.* v. *Halliday, ex parte Zadig*, the issue came before the House in the form of an application for habeas corpus. It was urged that the Regulation, under which a naturalized alien had been interned, was *ultra vires*. The House, with the dissent of Lord Shaw, decided that it was *intra vires*, that is to say, warranted by the language of the enabling Act. But in the 1939–45 war such care was taken, both by the Parliamentary draftsmen in the preparation of the enabling Act, and by the Home Office in the preparation of its regulations, that in 1941, when *Liversidge* v. *Anderson* came before the courts, the plaintiff, recognizing that he could not impeach the validity of Regulation 18B, posed as its champion. For, said he, the Regulation empowers the Secretary of State to order my detention if he has *reasonable cause* to believe that I have been engaged in acts prejudicial to the public safety; but I pin my case on those two emphasized words. It is for the courts alone to decide whether he

---

[10] The range of executive powers was widened by the Emergency Powers Act 1940, so as to give the executive, in effect, complete control over the persons, activities, and property of subjects, for securing the public safety.

had in fact reasonable cause for his belief. But the House, again with one dissentient, Lord Atkin, laid down that the matter fell entirely within the executive discretion of the Minister, and did not concern the courts at all. Extreme individualists took a gloomy view of this decision, regarding it as the Austerlitz of personal liberty; but their pessimism was shortly afterwards dispelled by palpable proof that the judiciary had in no sense 'sold the pass' to the executive, but will tolerate only such acts as are justified by the common law or by Statute. The act of a civil servant, who took it upon himself to intercept a letter from a detainee to the courts, was justified by neither; a High Court judge took occasion to animadvert on it in no uncertain terms; and the Home Secretary in the House of Commons, so far from attempting to defend the conduct of his ardent and anonymous subordinate, expressed an indignation at it amounting almost to horror.

In recent years there have been many examples of this imposition by the judges of the objective review of powers exercised by Ministers or other executive authorities. Thus, in the case of *Padfield* v. *Minister of Agriculture, Fisheries, and Food*, in 1968, a statutory power conferred upon the Minister to refer a complaint concerning a milk marketing scheme to a committee of investigation 'if the Minister in any case so directs' was held not to be proof against judicial review. The House of Lords considered that the Minister could only properly exercise his discretion in determining whether or not to refer such a complaint to the committee if he took into account matters which were relevant. As the Minister had given bad reasons for refusing so to refer the complaint which was at issue in *Padfield*, he was ordered to consider the complaint afresh. In *Secretary of State for Education and Science* v. *Tameside Metropolitan Borough Council*, in 1977, the Secretary of State was held by the Lords to have acted unreasonably in attempting to order a local education authority to implement a full scheme of comprehensive education to which it was opposed, for the local authority had already adequately discharged its duty under the legislation then in force to supply pupils with such instruction and training 'as may be desirable in view of their different ages, abilities and aptitudes'. And in *Laker Airways Ltd.* v. *Department of Trade*, also in 1977, the Court of Appeal granted a declaration that a government attempt to procure the revocation by the independent Civil Aviation

Authority of the plaintiff's licence to operate the celebrated 'Skytrain' cut-price trans-Atlantic air service was *ultra vires* and void. As in the *Tameside* case, a Minister's attempt to endow his political views with the force of law, while without full statutory authority for doing so, was defeated in the court.

These incidents serve as striking illustrations of that position of dignity to which British judges have attained, a position which is unique in the world. In expressing this estimate, an English writer is making no arrogant insular boast, putting forward no unsubstantiated claim, but rather accepting a tribute which is offered with embarrassing unanimity by foreign observers. How is the phenomenon to be explained? To such a question there can be no precise answer, but the secret lies in the method of appointment, and in the realization of a true judicial independence. We have avoided the standpoint of France and of Poland, that the Bench is a career alternative to the Bar, and so are spared the sight of a learned old *avocat* ostensibly pleading before, but actually hectoring, a young and inexperienced judge. We have consistently refused to be seduced by a false view of the essentials of democracy, which has led the majority of the States of America to adopt the system of an elective judiciary; we know that such a matter cannot safely be left to the collective vote, reliable as such a vote has in other matters shown itself to be, but have placed the appointment in the hands best calculated to shape the judicial Bench into an assembly of the best men. For the only road to the Bench lies through the Bar, or in the case of the Circuit Bench through both branches of the legal profession, and a judge comes to his office steeped in the traditions of his profession, which demand the highest standards of learning and of probity. Parliament has completed the good work by removing all temptation to disregard these high traditions. In an evil hour would Parliament remove the safeguards it has so wisely built round the judicial office.

Perhaps one last safeguard of individual liberties is provided by the institution of the Official Solicitor, who has the power to represent any person in any litigation, whether or not he has been asked to do so, where it appears to him that there is no other person competent or willing to act. Thus in 1972 the Official Solicitor successfully applied to the Court of Appeal to set aside an order by the National Industrial Relations Court (a court set up in 1971 and abolished in 1974) committing three trade union shop stewards to prison for failing to obey an order of the court. Although the three men seemed quite content to be martyred, the Official Solicitor, of his own accord, was able to show that the evidence of their disobedience fell short of the standard necessary in proceedings for contempt of court. Thus, even without the men's consent or knowledge, he secured their release.

10   Barristers and solicitors

In England, as in South Africa and some other countries, the legal profession is divided into barristers and solicitors. In the United States a legal firm will be composed of two types of member, those who advise the client and conduct all manner of administrative routine, and those who argue the case of the client in court. But in England the branches are entirely distinct, although some lawyers have at times argued in favour of their fusion. Legal firms consist entirely of solicitors; barristers are debarred by the rules of the profession from entering into partnerships with solicitors, or even with each other. The client comes into contact with a barrister only through the medium of a solicitor. It is possible, under certain conditions, for a solicitor to become a barrister, or a barrister a solicitor, and in recent years such a transfer has been much facilitated, but the rules of both branches provide that the one calling must be entirely relinquished before the other be undertaken. No man and no woman, therefore, can be at once a barrister and a solicitor. Though it is largely true that the functions of a solicitor are administrative and advisory, while those of a barrister are declamatory and dialectic, this does not express the whole truth. In this as in many other aspects of the English system there is a good deal of overlap, for there are solicitors who do a great deal of court work, and barristers who spend little or none of their time in court, especially those engaged mainly in advising on specialist points of law or the drawing up of legal documents. Since the United Kingdom became a member of the European Economic Community in 1973, conventions have been entered into enabling solicitors and barristers to practise in other Community countries, and to enable lawyers from such countries to practise in the U.K.

The governing bodies of both professions have it in mind that eventually there may be a common course of training and a common method of examining candidates for each profession. The possession of a law degree may also become a prerequisite to qualification. But as yet these aims seem unlikely to be wholly fulfilled for several years.

Solicitors

The education, examination, and discipline of solicitors are in the hands of the Law Society, founded by a charter of 1831, and at present regulated by a later charter of 1903. Membership of the Society is not compulsory, but all solicitors are subject to its control. The law applicable to solicitors was contained in a series of Acts starting in 1839, and now consolidated in the Solicitors Act 1974. In order to become a solicitor, a person must be duly admitted and enrolled. A request for admission is addressed to the Master of the Rolls, but a candidate cannot practise until he has obtained a certificate from the Law Society which must be annually renewed. The Solicitors Act now provides that regulations made by the Law Society for the education and training of persons seeking admission as solicitors must have the approval of the Lord Chancellor, the Lord Chief Justice, and the Master of the Rolls. These regulations have altered considerably in recent years, but at present the conditions for admission (subject to certain transitional provisions) are as follows:

(*a*) A candidate must complete an academic stage of training. This is normally done either by graduating with an approved law degree from a University or Polytechnic, or by passing the newly-created Common Professional Examination. This latter examination is already common to both branches of the legal profession, and replaces earlier separate Part I examinations. But the Law Society's Part I examination[1] remains as the academic stage of training available to some school-leavers. Courses in preparation for the Common Professional Examination are available at the College of Law in London, and at certain Polytechnics.

(*b*) He must then complete the professional or educational stage of his training. This comprises:

  (i) a period of service under articles; that is to say, work as a clerk in a solicitor's office;

  (ii) attendance at a recognized course of thirty-six weeks' duration; and

[1] Shortly to be replaced by a Solicitors' First Examination.

(iii) passing a Final Examination based on that course.

The period of articles is two years, at least eighteen months of which must be served after passing the Final Examination. The recognized course will be run by the College of Law and by a limited number of Polytechnics.

Solicitors have the right of audience in magistrates' courts, the County Court, and in certain proceedings before the Crown Court, e.g. in criminal proceedings on appeal from a magistrates' court where the solicitor had appeared for the defendant at his trial. They have no right of audience before the Judicial Committee of the Privy Council, the Court of Appeal, or High Court (except in bankruptcy matters and patent cases[2]). Curiously, solicitors may, with leave, be granted the right of audience in the House of Lords, because our ultimate court of appeal is technically a committee of a legislative chamber, rather than a court.[3] But in practice the right would never be sought or exercised.

Communications between solicitors and clients are of a strictly confidential character. Gifts made by a client to his solicitor are attended with a presumption of undue influence; that is to say, they can be recalled unless the solicitor can prove that he and his client were completely 'at arm's-length' in the matter. A solicitor who has been named as executor of his client's will cannot charge a fee for his services, including even his professional services, rendered in that capacity, unless the will contains a special clause known as the 'charging clause', and he must not insist on the insertion of such a clause. A solicitor can sue his client for his fees, and can be sued by him for negligence in the conduct of his business, though not, as a result of *Rondel* v. *Worsley* (1969), when acting as an advocate. The general regulation of scales of fees is in the hands of a committee consisting of the Master of the Rolls, the President of the Law Society, and others, to whom has been entrusted by the Solicitors Act 1974 the duty of making rules on this subject. No arrangement for 'contingent fees', such as is

[2] Right of audience in the Patents Court extends to both solicitors and patent agents.

[3] It is for the same reason that judges sitting in the House of Lords and the Judicial Committee of the Privy Council wear neither wigs nor gowns, though counsel appearing before them must be so attired, as is customary for both Bench and Bar in all other courts.

regular in the United States, that is to say for payment only in the event of a successful issue to an action, is countenanced in England. The trustees for the maintenance of the standard of professional honour are the Solicitors' Disciplinary Tribunal, composed of solicitors and lay members, appointed by the Master of the Rolls, who will take cognizance of professional misconduct by a solicitor, or of his conviction for an indictable crime. He can be struck off the roll, suspended, or obliged to pay costs. He can also apply for the removal of his name from the roll, and must do so as a first step on the road to becoming a barrister, just as a barrister who wishes to become a solicitor must first procure himself to be disbarred. Any complaints about the Law Society's handling of complaints against solicitors will be investigated by the Lay Observer, an independent officer appointed under the Solicitors Act 1974.

It is a trite saying that there are black sheep in every profession, but those in the solicitor's profession are happily few. A good solicitor becomes far more than an animated book of reference to his client; in nine cases out of ten he becomes his intimate personal friend, who can be trusted not only to respect confidence and implicitly carry out instructions, but to give much unobtrusive advice of a nature beneficial to his client and all his family. Countless must be the times in which a wise and levelheaded solicitor has restrained a client from being impelled by a foolish will or settlement; countless also those in which he has saved his client's fortunes by dissuading him from imprudent investment or profitless litigation. They are the couriers of the passage of life.

Barristers

The law applicable to a barrister is not statutory. His admission, education, and discipline are in the hands of the Benchers of the Inn of Court to which he belongs. He cannot practise until he has been 'called to the Bar' by one of these four Inns, the Inner Temple, the Middle Temple, Lincoln's Inn, and Gray's Inn. These four are unincorporated associations,[4] whose affairs are in no way subject to any governmental control. A candidate must first be admitted as a student at one of the Inns. He must then

[4] See p. 100.

normally 'keep terms', a condition satisfied by dining in the Hall of his Inn a given number of times. He must also pass the Bar Examinations, which are prescribed by a body to whom this task has been delegated by the four Inns, called the Council of Legal Education. This Council appoints Readers and Lecturers to give lectures on all the subjects, and examiners to conduct the examinations with the Readers and Lecturers. Instruction for the Bar Examinations is given only by the Inns of Court School of Law, which is run by the Council of Legal Education. Before he is permitted to practise, a barrister must also serve a period of twelve months as the pupil of a practising barrister of at least five years' standing (although he may actually start to practise after completing six of the twelve months' pupillage). The Bar Examinations are currently being altered by stages, and by 1980 they will be taken in one part, rather than two, and all candidates will already have to possess a law degree from a United Kingdom University or Polytechnic, or else have passed the Common Professional Examination, or an examination designed for non-law graduates for a Diploma in Law.

In 1974 a new central governing body to control and look after the interests of the whole profession was established, called the Senate of the Inns of Court and the Bar. This Senate replaces certain earlier bodies, and it controls the policy of the Council of Legal Education. It also appoints disciplinary tribunals to hear and determine any charge of professional misconduct against a barrister. If found guilty, any such barrister is reported to his Inn with a direction as to punishment, which may include a requirement to repay fees or that he be disbarred.

Barristers cannot sue for their fees, nor can they be sued for negligence when acting as advocates.[5] The first few years of a barrister's professional life, unless he had ample private means, used to be fraught with anxiety, for he can in no way advertise himself or seek for clients, nor can he enter into any professional

[5] But it would seem that there would be liability when acting other than as an advocate, i.e. in writing opinions, settling conveyances, etc.: see *Rondel* v. *Worsley* (1969). In relation to pre-trial work, a barrister's immunity from proceedings extends only to matters which are so intimately connected with the conduct of the cause at the trial that they may fairly be described as preliminary decisions affecting the manner of its conduct in court: *Saif Ali* v. *Sydney Mitchell & Co.* (1978).

partnership. He may supplement his professional income by adopting other activities as side-lines, though some activities, such as trading, are forbidden by the rules of the profession, and those which are permitted, such as journalism, may tend to take up a lot of his time. But many young barristers now receive financial assistance from their Inns at the beginning of their careers, especially in the form of grants to help cover the necessary expense of pupillage. Also the existence since the Second World War of free legal aid for many of the less wealthy clients has meant that nowadays newly qualified barristers are often able to make a good living during their first year or two in practice, for the volume of litigation has increased enormously during the past thirty years, and their later financial prospects are good. Some senior barristers are appointed as Queen's Counsel, and will normally be briefed only to argue the more important cases in court.

The standard of professional honour is as high among barristers as among solicitors. The duality of the system has its disadvantages, of which perhaps the chief used to be that a seat on the professional Bench was for the most part open to barristers alone. But even this rule has been breached since the Courts Act 1971, for now, in addition to the post of stipendiary magistrate which was already open to a solicitor, the way to the Circuit Bench is also open.[6] On the whole the system works well and is unlikely to be changed in its essentials.

We have now followed a path which has taken us through many centuries of legal development to the present day. There is nothing new in the existence of modern criticism of lawyers, the courts, or of various aspects of the law itself. Our legal history is one long procession of experiment and change, with probably the most striking periods of such change in the legal system being the twelfth, nineteenth and twentieth centuries. Law does not exist as an end in itself. It is merely an instrument to serve the needs of a law-abiding and peaceful society. As those needs change, and particularly as society becomes more just and fair-minded, law reform is required. Those who castigate the law as out-dated, and

[6] See p. 112.

lawyers as essentially conservative, miss the point that law reform can scarcely take place until a need for it has been shown. Legislation may sometimes be speculative in the sense that it is hoped by Parliament that it will meet a future need, but events often give the lie to these hopes. More often a fault in the law is exposed by litigation not previously foreseen, or else the wishes of society at large have altered. An example of Parliamentary response to change of public opinion was the creation for the first time of judicial dissolution of marriage, commonly known as divorce, by the Matrimonial Causes Act 1857, as mentioned above in Chapter 8. Few would doubt that this legislation was demanded by the people of that time, but inevitably it took some years for the demand to become clear in such a way that Parliament was prepared to act upon it.

Our courts and lawyers are the machinery and instruments for effecting the law. In this book we have attempted to show how, in response to society's needs, they have evolved and developed over the centuries. It would be idle to suggest that today they have reached perfection. But no one should underestimate the efforts made over the years by legislators, judges, and legal practitioners to meet society's requirements. In these efforts they have in recent decades been open to advice from academic writers and teachers. We can be confident that the legal system will continue to respond to adequately expressed demands for reform, and that it will remain as flexible and inventive as circumstances warrant.

Further reading

There are many books which may be consulted with profit on various aspects of the English courts and their history. Most of the historical works are concerned with the whole area of legal history, such as Baker, *Introduction to English Legal History* (Butterworth); Plucknett, *A Concise History of the Common Law* (Butterworth); and Milsom, *Historical Foundations of the Common Law* (Butterworth). But other works specialize upon particular aspects of substantive law, and include Maitland, *Forms of Action at Common Law* (Cambridge), which is a short book containing the late Professor Maitland's lectures at Cambridge on the origins of what is now the law of contract, of tort, and of land; Simpson, *A History of the Law of Contract* (Oxford), and *An Introduction to the History of the Land Law* (Oxford); Plucknett, *Edward I and Criminal Law* (Cambridge), and *The Legislation of Edward I* (Oxford); Powicke, *King Henry III and the Lord Edward* (Oxford); and Green, *Henry the Second* (Twelve English Statesmen Series, Macmillan). Two books by the late C. H. S. Fifoot, *English Law and its Background* (Bell) and *History and Sources of the Common Law* (Stevens), are particularly useful in that they present many complex legal developments in a most attractive literary style. An American view of English legal history can be gained from Ames, *Lectures on Legal History* (Harvard Universtiy Press). Light upon general English history as a background for legal developments can be gained from the objective Trevelyan, *History of England* (Longman) or the more idiosyncratic Rowse, *The Spirit of English History* (Jonathan Cape). Specific works upon the history of the legal system and of the courts include Ensor, *Courts and Judges* (Oxford); Lovell, *English Constitutional and Legal History* (Oxford); and some of the writings of the great Sir William Holdsworth, notably *Essays in Law and History*, Chapters 3 and 4 (Oxford), *Sources and Literature of English Law* (Oxford), and volume 1 of the monumental *History of English Law* (Methuen). A classic account of the whole of English law as it was in the mid-eighteenth century is to be found in the four volumes of Blackstone, *Commentaries on the Laws of England* (Sweet), first published in 1783.

A good introduction to jurisprudence or the philosophy of law, albeit now a little dated, is to be found in Vinogradoff, *Common Sense in Law* (Home University Library, Oxford). A more detailed work is Gray, *Nature and Sources of the Law* (Columbia University Press), while an appreciation of the influence of the notable late eighteenth- and early nineteenth-century philosopher Bentham can be gained from his *Theory of Legislation* (Kegan Paul). The doctrine of sovereignty in law is expounded in Austin, *The Province of Jurisprudence Determined*, Lectures 1, 5, and 6, which is studied most conveniently in H. L. A. Hart's edition (Weidenfeld and Nicolson). But perhaps the most balanced modern account of the meaning and place of sovereignty is to be found in Professor Hart's own *The Concept of Law* (Clarendon Law Series, Oxford). The most celebrated analysis of the essential structure of a legal system as it grows up is Maine, *Ancient Law* (World's Classics, Oxford), which is as valid today as it was when first published in 1861.

The classic nineteenth-century account of the English Constitution is to be found in Bagehot, *The English Constitution* (World's Classics, Oxford), while comparison with the growth of the United States Constitution can be gleaned from Hamilton, Madison, and Jay, *The Federalist* (1787), or from Pound, *The Development of Constitutional Guarantees of Liberty* (Yale/Oxford). Books on specific aspects of constitutional history include Pasquet, *The Origins of the House of Commons* (Laffan's tr., Cambridge); Pollard, *The Evolution of Parliament* (Yale University Press); McKechnie, *Magna Carta* (MacLehose); and Richardson and Sayles, *The Governance of Medieval England: from the Conquest to Magna Carta* (Edinburgh University Press). More comprehensive accounts of constitutional history are Chrimes, *English Constitutional History* (OPUS, Oxford); Maitland, *The Constitutional History of England* (Cambridge); Stephenson and Marcham, *Sources of English Constitutional History* (Harper); and Taswell-Langmead, *English Constitutional History* (Sweet and Maxwell); as well as the book by Lovell mentioned above. By contrast to the history of the Constitution, some ideas for future constitutional reforms can be found in Hood Phillips, *Reform of the Constitution* (Chatto v Windus: Charles

Knight), published 1970.

Today there is an ever-growing list of books dealing with the subject of modern constitutional law, and of its special offshoot administrative law. All the modern textbooks are regularly kept up-to-date with the appearance of new editions. The subject has developed and changed so rapidly that many of the older works can now be ignored, but Newsam, *The Home Office* (Allen and Unwin) is still a useful monograph, and there is also some value to be gained from studying two books by the late Sir Ivor Jennings, *The British Constitution* (Cambridge) and *The Law and the Constitution* (University of London Press); as well as Allen, *Law and Orders* (Stevens); Dicey, *Introduction to the Study of the Law of the Constitution* (Macmillan), which contains his famous lectures first delivered at Oxford in the late nineteenth century; Wheare, *The Constitutional Structure of the Commonwealth* (Oxford); and two reports of Government Committees which have had a marked effect upon the development of administrative law in the present century, namely *Report of the Committee on Ministers' Powers* (H.M. Stationery Office, 1932, reprinted. Cmnd. 4060), and *Report of the Committee on Administrative Tribunals and Enquiries*, commonly known as the Franks Committee (H.M. Stationery Office, 1957. Cmnd. 218). Yardley, *Introduction to British Constitutional Law* (Butterworth) can be used as a short work covering the whole field in an introductory way and pointing towards larger books on the subject. There are three main larger textbooks, namely Hood Phillips, *Constitutional and Administrative Law* (Sweet and Maxwell); de Smith, *Constitutional and Administrative Law* (Penguin); and E. C. S. Wade and Phillips, *Constitutional and Administrative Law* (Longman). Wheare, *Modern Constitutions* (OPUS, Oxford) provides a useful general essay; and Keir and Lawson, *Cases in Constitutional Law* (Oxford) contains valuable source material. A concise introduction to administrative law can be found in Foulkes, *Introduction to Administrative Law* (Butterworth); and the rather older Griffith and Street, are H. W. R. Wade, *Administrative Law* (Oxford); Garner, *Administrative Law* (Butterworth); and the rather older Griffith and Street, *Principles of Administrative Law* (Pitman).

Perhaps one of the most useful books for those first setting out upon legal study, providing guidance to terminology, libraries and other basic materials, is Williams, *Learning the Law* (Stevens); while an interesting account of the growth of academic legal education in England can be found in Hanbury, *The Vinerian Chair and Legal Education* (Blackwells). Ethics of the legal profession and of the judiciary are discussed in Boulton, *Conduct and Etiquette at the Bar* (Butterworth); Cecil, *The English Judge* (Stevens); and Keeton, *English Law: The Judicial Contribution* (David and Charles).

The elements of substantive English law today are set out in James, *Introduction to English Law* (Butterworth); Hood Phillips and Hudson, *A First Book of English Law* (Sweet and Maxwell); Hanbury and Maudsley, *Modern Equity* (Stevens); and more generally but concisely in Geldart, *Elements of English Law*, edition by D. C. M. Yardley (OPUS, Oxford). Those interested in local government may consult Cross, *Principles of Local Government Law* (Sweet and Maxwell); Hart and Hart, *Introduction to the Law of Local Government and Administration*, edition by Sir W. O. Hart and J. F. Garner (Sweet and Maxwell); or the more dated Jennings, *Principles of Local Government Law* (University of London Press).

The only major book which deals in part with the history of the legal system as well as its present pattern is Radcliffe and Cross, *The English Legal System* (Butterworth). Of the works devoted to the modern court system, those which are no longer quite up-to-date include Rudd, *The English Legal System* (Butterworth); Archer, *The Queen's Courts* (Penguin); and Milton, *The English Magistracy* (OPUS, Oxford). Good accurate accounts can, however, be found in Jackson, *The Machinery of Justice in England* (Cambridge); Eddey, *The English Legal System* (Sweet and Maxwell); Kiralfy, *The English Legal System* (Sweet and Maxwell); Scott, *The Crown Court* (Butterworth); Friesen and Scott, *English Criminal Justice* (Institute of Judicial Administration, University of Birmingham); and Walker and Walker, *The English Legal System* (Butterworth), which is the largest work on the subject. Useful collections of source material can be consulted in Wilson, *Cases and Materials on the English Legal System* (Sweet and Maxwell); and Zander, *Cases and Materials on the English Legal System* (Weidenfeld and Nicolson).

Index